CITE THIS BOOK

THUS:

first tuesday

Ethics, Agency, Fair Housing and Trust Funds

First Edition

Cutoff Dates:
Legal editing of this book was
completed January 30, 2004

First Edition
1st printing March 2004

Printed in the United States of America

Editorial Staff

Legal Editor/Publisher:
Fred Crane

Managing Editor:
Brandi Ortega

Editorial Assistant:
Joseph Duong

Editors:
Ai M. Kelley
Jenice Tam

Comments or suggestions to:
first tuesday, P.O. Box 20069, Riverside, CA 92516
e-mail: editorial@firsttuesdayonline.com
www.firsttuesdayonline.com

Table Of Contents

SECTION A

Ethics

SECTION B

Agency

SECTION C

Fair Housing

SECTION D

Table of Forms

SECTION A

ETHICS

Chapter 1

Conflicts of interest in brokerage

This chapter examines the unlawful conduct and unprofessional behavior of real estate licensees when acting as an agent or as a principal in real estate related transactions.

Defining unlawful conduct

The Real Estate Commissioner is empowered by the state legislature to adopt regulations for the administration and enforcement of the Real Estate Law and Subdivided Lands Act. [Calif. Business and Professions Code §10080]

Both the **Real Estate Law** (Business and Professions Code §10000 et seq.) and the **Department of Real Estate Regulations** act to protect consumers of *services rendered* by real estate licensees. Thus, the public is assured real estate licensees will be honest, truthful and of good reputation, in a word, *ethical.*

Webster's Dictionary defines *ethics* as a "system or code of morals of a particular...group, profession, etc." [Webster's New World Dictionary, Third College Edition (1988)]

Black's Law Dictionary describes ethical conduct as "...professionally right or befitting; conforming to professional standards." [Black's Law Dictionary, Fifth Edition (1979)]

Thus, ethics and professionalism are synonymous. The real estate profession should demand nothing less than completely ethical behavior from fellow licensees, whether dealing between themselves or with members of the public as principals or as agents. Peer pressure imposed by fellow licensees generally produces corrected conduct by the offending licensee at an early stage, before continuing and evolving bad conduct causes the Department of Real Estate (DRE) to become involved.

Whenever a real estate broker or sales agent acts unprofessionally, he subjects himself to:

- liability to offended principals for money damages caused by his conduct (the loss of a commission, or worse); and

- disciplinary action by the DRE resulting in possible license suspension or revocation.

For real estate licensees to conduct themselves properly, they must be thoroughly familiar with the Real Estate Commissioner's regulations and apply lawful principles in the conduct of their practice.

The guidelines comprising a study of proper conduct for individuals who are licensed by the DRE include:

- California Business and Professions Code §10176; and

- California Business and Professions Code §10177.

Unlawful conduct, also called unethical conduct, improper conduct and unprofessional conduct, is generally defined as engaging in *fraud* or *dishonest dealing* or conduct which would have warranted denial of an application for a real estate license. [B & P C §§10176; 10177]

The following is a review of improper conduct that a broker or sales agent must avoid.

Misrepresenting real estate values for brokerage or personal gain

Brokers and sales agents must not misrepresent to an owner the likely **market value** of an owner's property to:

- obtain a listing;

- acquire an interest in the property for their own account; or

- induce a prospective buyer to make an offer to purchase the property.

For example, a seller lists his property for sale with a broker based on the broker's representations that he will be able to obtain a specific price for the property.

The broker locates a potential buyer willing to purchase the property at the listed price.

The broker does not disclose the existence of the buyer or the offer to the seller. Instead, the broker tells the seller he is unable to locate a buyer at the seller's asking price. The broker tells the seller he should consider lowering the price.

Relying on his broker's advice, the seller lowers his asking price.

Later, the broker again represents to the seller he cannot find a buyer. The broker then offers to purchase the property himself. The seller agrees and the broker opens escrow as a principal — the buyer — and takes title to the property on closing.

Immediately after escrow closes, the broker resells the property at the seller's original asking price.

Here, the broker intentionally misrepresented the market value of the property and the presence of buyers to induce the seller to reduce the asking price to an amount below the property's fair market value.

Having caused the listing price to be reduced while acting as an agent, the broker proceeds to purchase the property for his own account and resell it at a profit in excess of the percentage fee discussed with the seller.

However, a broker may not put his own interests for personal gain before those of his client. A broker must fully disclose the status of existing buyers, the price they will pay and his total earnings on the transaction proposed to the client. [**Rattray** v. **Scudder** (1946) 28 C2d 214]

If a broker intends to profit as a principal in a transaction, he must either avoid acting as an agent at any time or fully disclose his knowledge of activities if he does act as an agent.

Now consider the responsibilities owed to a seller by a buyer who also happens to be a licensed broker. Representations made to the seller by the broker concerning the price obtainable for a property must be accurate — even though the broker is acting as a principal and buying the property for his own account rather than acting in the capacity of the seller's listing broker. [**Smith** v. **Zak** (1971) 20 CA3d 785]

A licensee cannot, either by partial suppression, concealment or deliberate misrepresentation, make untruthful and misleading statements about the market value of a property, whether acting as an agent or a principal. [B & P C §§10176(a); 10177(f); Calif. Civil Code §2230]

Now consider a broker who is employed by a seller under a listing agreement to locate buyers for real estate. The listing agreement includes a purchase option in favor of the broker, exercisable during the listing period, called an *option listing*.

The *option listing* gives the broker an option to buy the property at a predetermined price if the property does not sell during the listing period.

Thus, the broker becomes both principal (holding the option) and agent (employed to locate buyers). The potential for misrepresentation increases when these highly conflicting relationships coexist.

For example, a seller's broker has a listing coupled with a purchase option. The broker might locate a buyer who will pay a price in excess of the option price, and then exercise his option to buy the property at the lesser option price and resell the property to the buyer without informing the seller about the buyer.

Also, a seller's broker may legitimately decide to purchase the listed property with the intention of later reselling it at a profit. Later, when the property resells at a higher price, the seller will likely seek to recover the broker's profit, claiming the broker failed to diligently market the property under the listing agreement.

Likewise, the broker exercising a purchase option may overlook his need to inform the seller of all the inquiries he received on the listing.

However, a broker cannot exercise his option to buy property listed under an option listing unless he first fulfills his agency obligation to the seller. The broker must first make a full disclosure of the property's fair market value and of all offers he receives on the property before exercising a purchase option he holds. [*Rattray*, supra]

Investigate property conditions before representing them as fact

Now consider a broker who advertises a home as having been designed by a famous architect. Relying on the broker's representation, a buyer enters into a purchase agreement. A further-approval contingency that allows the buyer to either confirm the broker's representations or cancel the transaction is not included in the purchase agreement. The broker's representation is considered a fact.

Before closing escrow, the buyer learns that no evidence exists to prove the home was designed by the famous architect. The broker recommends the buyer cancel escrow, which the buyer refuses to do.

After escrow closes, the buyer seeks to recover money from the broker for the diminished value of the home due to the misrepresentation concerning the design of the home.

The broker claims the buyer is not entitled to recover any money since the buyer proceeded to **close escrow** with the knowledge that no proof existed that the architect designed the home.

However, the broker is liable for the diminished value of the home due to the architectural misrepresentation. The buyer relied on the broker's representation at the time the purchase price was set and the purchase agreement was entered into with the seller, not later as would have occurred under a contingency provision.

A buyer who relies on a broker's *unconditional representations* — no contingency to confirm or cancel — to enter into a real estate purchase agreement and discovers the representations are incorrect prior to closing, may close escrow and later recover his losses suffered as a result of the misrepresentation. [**Jue** v. **Smiser** (1994) 23 CA4th 312]

To instruct brokers and sales agents, the *Jue* court observed:

"Our decision should encourage sellers and their representatives to investigate and learn the true facts pertaining to real property before it is offered for sale." [Jue, *supra*, 23 CA4th at p. 246]

On the other hand, the broker who fails to first confirm a representation he makes about the property can avoid liability by including a further-approval contingency that allows the buyer to cancel if the representation cannot be confirmed.

When listing, represent the existence of an offer only if one exists

A broker and his agents may not represent the existence of a buyer for a property to induce a seller to list property when no buyer is known to exist.

For example, a broker tells an owner, whose property is in foreclosure, he has a buyer for the property. However, a buyer does not exist.

The broker's representation about the existence of a buyer induces the seller to sign an exclusive right-to-sell listing agreement employing the broker to locate a buyer.

The seller relies on the broker to produce a buyer and close a sale of the property before he loses it in foreclosure.

However, the broker makes no effort to market the property other than the publication and dissemination of information on the property through a Multiple Listing Service (MLS).

Ultimately, the broker does not produce a buyer and the seller loses the property in a foreclosure sale.

As a result, the broker is liable to the seller for the loss of the seller's equity.

Also, the broker's license may be suspended or permanently revoked. [B & P C §§10176(a),(b); 10177(c),(g),(j)]

If the broker *has* a buyer, he should:

1. Enter into a listing agreement with the buyer. [See **first tuesday** Form 103]

2. Prepare a written offer which is signed by the buyer and presented to the seller;

    and

3. Provide for the brokerage fee in the body of the written offer signed by the buyer. [See **first tuesday** Form 150, §14]

If a broker has initially undertaken the task of locating property for a buyer, he is well advised to *formalize the agency* relationship and his expectation of a brokerage fee by using a buyer's listing agreement, rather than seeking a listing from the seller and creating a dual agency. [**Phillippe** v. **Shapell Industries, Inc.** (1987) 43 C3d 1247]

Fees are determined by each broker individually

A broker and his agents must not state or imply they are prevented by a law, a regulation, or rules of a trade organization from negotiating the amount of the brokerage fee.

For example, an association of real estate licensees openly encourages uniform fee rates based on the need to maintain a minimum level of income necessary to support a professional lifestyle for its members.

The association publishes literature using examples of a 6% brokerage fee on residential sales and an equal split of fees between listing and selling brokers.

Further, the association requires its MLS members to include both sides of the brokerage fee in each publication of the listed property.

An MLS broker decides to compete with the fixed rates set by the association by offering to provide the same brokerage services for a lower fee, referred to as a *discount broker*. Also, he offers to share 40% of his fee with any selling broker who produces a buyer at the listed price and on the listed terms.

The association then adopts a policy stating the fee split published in the MLS by other listing brokers can be altered as against any one selling broker, if advance notice of the altered fee split is given to the other broker.

A listing broker sends the competing broker a letter that states the brokerage fee the competing broker will receive should he sell one of the broker's listings will be less than the share published in the MLS.

Another listing broker advises the competing broker that when he complies with the current brokerage fees as published in the association's literature, the listing broker will split the brokerage fee equally as he does with all other selling brokers who conform.

The association members also inform home-owners listed with the competing broker that their property will not be shown to prospective buyers while it remains listed with the competing "discount" broker.

The competing broker, acting as a selling agent, submits an offer to purchase property listed in the MLS. The MLS listing provides for the brokerage fee to be split equally between the two brokers.

However, the listing broker insists on retaining a greater percentage of the fee since the competing broker does not follow the "accepted" brokerage fee guidelines.

The competing broker files an arbitration complaint with the association as required for resolution of disputes among its members. The complaint is arbitrated and the arbitration board holds the listing broker is to receive the higher percentage of the fee on the property sold by the competing broker. Further, the competing broker is assessed the costs of arbitration.

Eventually, economic pressure by association members successfully forces the competing broker to raise the brokerage fee he charges the public and to split the fee equally with selling brokers in the local MLS.

A complaint is filed against the association for its actions by the State of California. The association and its members are charged with having engaged in the illegal practice of price fixing by adopting and enforcing policies to discriminate against competing brokers.

As a result, the association is held to have violated unlawful competition statutes and restraints on trade through the practice of illegal price fixing. The association is ordered to pay statutory penalties for its conduct. [**People** v. **National Association of Realtors** (1981) 120 CA3d 459]

Misrepresenting a licensee's employment with a broker

A sales agent may not misrepresent his employment relationship with a broker or a broker's responsibility for his conduct.

For example, a sales agent, while employed by a broker, negotiates two real estate loans for an investor.

Later, the sales agent is terminated as an employee of the broker. The sales agent then contacts the same investor and arranges for the origination of another real estate loan.

The investor is not aware that the sales agent is not presently employed by a broker.

The annual interest rate yield on the real estate loan arranged by the sales agent exceeds the 11th District Federal Reserve Bank rate by more than 5%.

After the loan is originated, the borrower claims the excessive interest rate makes the loan usurious and limits the investor's recovery to the principal investment in the loan.

However, a loan secured by real estate is not usurious if the sales agent arranging the loan is an agent of a licensed broker who is acting on behalf of either the borrower or the lender when the loan is made. [Calif. Constitution Article XV]

Thus, the loan arranged by the unemployed sales agent is usurious as no broker *made or arranged the loan*. Accordingly, the sales agent is liable to the investor for the loss of interest on the loan since he failed to disclose to the investor that he was not employed by a licensed broker when the loan was made, a misrepresentation called an *omission*. [**Dierenfield** v. **Stabile** (1988) 198 CA3d 126]

Disclose agent's or relative's interest in the property sold

A seller's broker must disclose to his seller-client the extent of any direct or indirect interest the broker expects to acquire in the property, or whether a family member, a business owned by the broker, or any other person holding a special relationship with the broker will acquire any interest in the seller's property.

For example, a broker's brother-in-law offers to buy property from an estate through a probate proceeding under a purchase agreement stating the broker is to receive a fee.

The broker does not disclose to any representative of the estate or to the probate court that the buyer is his brother-in-law.

The probate court confirms the sale, including the brokerage fee.

The broker opens two escrows. The first escrow facilitates the sale from the estate to the broker's brother-in-law.

The second escrow transfers title of the property from the brother-in-law to a company in which the broker holds a majority share of stock. The probate sale closes and the broker receives his fee.

Here, the broker is not entitled to retain the brokerage fee he received from the estate. The estate is also entitled to either recover any reduction in price or set the sale aside due to the misrepresentation of the broker's agency.

A broker cannot act for more than one party in a transaction, including himself, without disclosing his dual role. [B & P C §10176(d)]

Also, a broker has an affirmative duty to disclose to a seller his agencies and any conflicting relationship with the buyer, even if the seller fails to inquire about the true nature of the broker's relationship with the buyer.

Further, failure to disclose a broker's personal interest as a buyer in a transaction when he is also acting **as an agent** of the seller constitutes grounds for discipline by the Real Estate Commissioner. [**Whitehead** v. **Gordon** (1970) 2 CA3d 659]

In another example, a seller, acting on a broker's advice as to the estimated value of his real estate, retains the broker to find a buyer for the property.

The broker and seller enter into a *net listing* agreement.

Under the net listing, the seller agrees to take a fixed sum of money as the net proceeds for his equity should the property sell. Also, the net listing provides for the broker to receive all further sums paid on the price as his brokerage fee.

The broker arranges a sale of the property to his daughter and son-in-law. On close of the transaction, the broker receives his brokerage fee.

The seller is not informed of the broker's relationship with the buyer. On discovery of the relationship, the seller demands a return of the brokerage fee. The broker claims the seller cannot recover the brokerage fee since the seller only bargained for a fixed amount for his property under the net listing agreement.

However, a broker employed under any type of listing has an obligation to voluntarily disclose to his seller any special relationship he may have with the buyer. The seller, unaware of the family relationship between his broker and the buyer, can recover the brokerage fee he paid to the broker. [**Sierra Pacific Industries** v. **Carter** (1980) 104 CA3d 579]

Disclose agent's or relative's ownership interest in property sold

A broker acting as an agent on behalf of a buyer must disclose to the buyer the nature and extent of any direct or indirect interest he holds in the property sold.

Conversely, a broker acting solely as a principal for his own behalf need not disclose the existence of his brokerage license when buying (or selling) property. The broker has no conflict since he is not also acting as an agent in the transaction.

For example, a broker acting as an agent of a buyer shows the buyer several properties, one of which is owned by the broker, along with others vested in the name of a limited liability company (LLC). The broker does not inform the buyer of his indirect ownership interest in the property.

The buyer later decides to purchase the property in which the broker has an interest.

Since the broker is the buyer's agent, the broker learns the buyer will pay a higher price for the property than the price specified in the buyer's original offer. Thus, the broker presents the buyer with a counteroffer from the LLC which provides for a higher selling price. The buyer accepts the counteroffer.

Thus, the broker profits both from the amount paid by the buyer to buy the property and the amount received as his brokerage fee — the result of a conflict of interest.

Had the buyer known the broker held an ownership interest in the property, he might have retained a different broker to represent his interests.

Here, the broker has a duty to timely disclose his ownership interest in the property to his client. The information is a material fact since the broker's conflict of interest might affect the client's decisions concerning acquisition of the property.

However, a broker acting solely as a principal in the sale of his own property is not restricted by agency requirements. The broker should represent himself as being a seller exclusively, rather than a seller who is paying himself a (taxable) fee for also acting as a broker in the transaction. [**Robinson** v. **Murphy** (1979) 96 CA3d 763]

When the broker-seller receives a brokerage fee on the sale of his own property or property he purchases for his own account, he is subject to real estate agency requirements.

For example, a broker owns a residence which violates safety requirements for occupation due to defects in the foundation.

The broker does not tell the buyer about the foundation defects.

In addition to the price received for the property, the broker-seller pays himself a brokerage fee on the transaction.

The buyer later discovers he must demolish the residence and rebuild with an adequate foundation. The buyer obtains a money judgment against the broker for breach of his agency duty to disclose a *known defect* that caused the buyer to take a loss.

The broker is unable to pay the money judgment. The buyer seeks payment from the DRE Recovery Fund.

Recovery is received from the DRE Recovery Fund since the seller also acted as a broker in the transaction. The broker's license is also suspended. Before the broker can reactivate his license, he must reimburse the DRE fund. [**Prichard** v. **Reitz** (1986) 170 CA3d 465]

Disclose to the client any interest the licensee holds in a business referral

A broker must voluntarily inform a client of any significant interest he or his agents hold in a business that is recommended to the client by the broker's office for the performance of services or the sale of products.

For example, a broker arranges a loan for a borrower. The lender making the loan is the broker's sister.

The broker, however, funds the loan himself by depositing his personal funds into his sister's account.

In essence, the broker is the lender.

The borrower is not aware of the relationship between the broker and the lender or of the true source of the loan funds.

Here, the broker fails in his duty to disclose his dual representation in acting as both a broker and as the maker of the loan. The broker's actions constitute grounds for discipline by the Real Estate Commissioner. [**Tushner** v. **Savage** (1963) 219 CA2d 71]

A licensee cannot act for more than one party in a transaction without the prior knowledge or consent of all parties. [B & P C §10176(d)]

Chapter 2

Document disclosures and alterations

This chapter discusses the effects estimates, postdated checks, creditworthiness and document alterations have on the validity of documents.

Closing costs to be estimated in good faith

A broker and his sales agents must avoid inducing any buyer or seller to make or accept an offer to purchase or sell real estate by giving them an **underestimate** of the probable closing costs on the transaction.

For example, a buyer may rely on the representations of his broker for the amount of funds needed to close escrow on the purchase agreement negotiated by the broker.

When a buyer makes an offer, the financial consequences of the seller's acceptance (and resulting binding agreement) and the completion of the purchase on close of escrow are presented to the buyer in the form of a cost sheet. [See **first tuesday** Form 311]

With the use of a **cost sheet**, the purchase price and all transactional closing costs to be borne by the buyer, as well as the buyer's source of funds, is clearly and completely disclosed by the buyer's broker.

As for sellers, a seller's net sheet is prepared by the seller's broker and reviewed with the seller to accurately produce the financial "bottom line" — the net proceeds he will receive on closing the transaction — should the seller decide to list the property for sale or accept an offer. [See **first tuesday** Form 310]

The **seller's net sheet** is prepared and delivered to the seller on:

- the presentation of a listing agreement; and
- the submission of a purchase agreement offer for acceptance.

Sellers are greatly influenced to sell property by their broker's representation of the net proceeds they will receive from a proposed transaction and what form the proceeds will take — cash, paper or an exchange of equities.

The figures entered on the seller's net sheet must be as accurate as reasonably possible. A resourceful agent will be able to produce close estimates.

When the accuracy of a figure entered on a disclosure statement is an estimate, such as the cost of a termite clearance, the words "approximation" or "approximately" should highlight the uncertainty.

Estimates are required to be made in *good faith* to eliminate an agent's temptation to guess. Also, an estimation cannot be given if the actual amount is already known.

Good faith deposit disclosure

Brokers who accept a good faith deposit with a purchase offer must make sufficient disclosures to sellers about the deposit to avoid deceiving the seller as to the form, amount, handling or ownership of the buyer's good faith deposit.

For example, a buyer gives his broker a good faith deposit in the form of a personal check and signs an offer to purchase property.

The check is postdated. The buyer does not have sufficient funds on deposit to cover the check.

The purchase agreement states the check for the good faith deposit is to be deposited when the offer is accepted. The purchase agreement does not disclose the check is postdated. Specifically, nothing written, except the check, states the check is not of the same date as the purchase agreement.

The purchase agreement offer is presented to the seller. However, the seller is not handed a copy of the check nor otherwise informed that the check for the good faith deposit is postdated.

The buyer's offer to purchase the property is accepted by the seller and delivered to the buyer.

Later, the seller discovers the check is postdated. The seller then withdraws his acceptance and refuses to sell, claiming the postdated check is a promissory note.

The buyer and the broker seek to recover their losses, claiming the seller breached by cancelling the transaction.

However, a postdated check is not the same as a check. A check is payable on demand. Conversely, a **postdated check** is merely a promise to pay on or after the date on the check. Thus, the broker's failure to disclose important facts regarding the good faith deposit accompanying the buyer's offer is a misrepresentation charged to the broker and the buyer.

An agreement is *voidable* and may be cancelled by the seller when acceptance is obtained through a misrepresentation of the buyer or the other party's broker. [Calif. Civil Code §1689(b)(2)]

Thus, the seller can cancel the agreement. The broker failed to disclose the check evidencing the good faith deposit was a postdated check. Accordingly, neither the buyer nor the broker can collect money losses for the seller's refusal to perform — the agreement was voidable due to the nondisclosure of the check as a promissory note.

The predated condition should have been entered in the receipt of deposit section of the purchase agreement and a copy of the postdated check handed to the seller. The broker would retain the check as trust funds. [**Wilson** v. **Lewis** (1980) 106 CA3d 802]

Buyer's ability to pay a carryback note

A broker and his agents will not misrepresent to a carryback seller a buyer's financial ability to perform the terms and conditions of the carryback note and trust deed.

For example, a listing broker locates a buyer willing to purchase his seller's property.

The broker advises the seller that the buyer is financially qualified to make the large cash down payment that the seller requires before he will provide carryback financing for the remainder of the purchase price.

Relying on the broker's representations as to the buyer's financial qualifications, the seller agrees to carry back paper to facilitate the sale.

Before escrow closes, the buyer advises the broker he does not have the downpayment money and will need to obtain a loan to fund the closing.

The broker does not advise the seller of the buyer's lack of downpayment funds. Further, the broker makes the buyer the loan necessary to fund the down payment.

Escrow closes and the buyer takes title to the property. Soon the buyer defaults on his payments on the carryback note held by the seller.

The seller then discovers the buyer obtained a loan from the broker for the down payment and that the broker knew the buyer was financially unstable due to a lack of funds prior to closing.

Here, the broker is liable for the seller's losses on the carryback note. The broker failed to disclose the buyer's adverse financial status to the seller prior to closing the sale. The seller's broker has an agency duty to advise the seller about the buyer's financial capability (net worth) and the likelihood he will timely pay on the carryback note (credit analysis). [**Ziswasser** v. **Cole** (1985) 164 CA3d 417]

A seller willing to carry paper needs to know if the prospective buyer has an incentive to protect his equity and is able to make the payments. A buyer's willingness and ability to make future payments is of great concern to carryback sellers, especially since carryback financing is most prevalent during a falling real estate market (just the market which produces more unqualified buyers).

The seller's broker has a duty to accurately provide a carryback seller with any credit information he possesses on the buyer, and to either further investigate or advise the seller to further investigate the buyer's creditworthiness under a further-approval contingency.

More specifically, brokers have an affirmative duty to make a written financial disclosure to the carryback seller about the buyer's creditworthiness on the sale of one-to-four unit residential property. [See **first tuesday** Form 300]

The credit disclosure is mandated on all sales of one-to-four unit residential property when the seller is to carry back any part of the sales price. [CC §2956 et seq.]

A broker's misrepresentation or omission of a buyer's future ability and willingness to meet the terms and conditions of a seller carryback note not only subjects the broker to money damages, but to the possible suspension or revocation of his license as well. [Calif. Business and Professions Code §§10176, 10177(c),(g),(j)]

Defacing a previously signed document

A broker or sales agent must not alter a document once it is signed without that party's prior consent.

Consider a broker who submits a buyer's signed offer to a seller. The seller will not accept all the terms contained in the offer, but will sell if the buyer agrees to some "minor" changes, including a larger down payment and a shorter escrow period.

The broker strikes out the downpayment amount and the escrow period provisions by crossing them out on the purchase agreement form signed by the buyer, an activity called *defacing*. The seller's changes are then entered by *interlineation* to replace the original entries. The seller signs the acceptance provision on the form, and initials and dates all the changes.

The original offer as altered on its face is then presented to the buyer for his approval by also initialing and dating the changes.

The altering of a signed document is wrong. The broker should have prepared, and the seller should have signed, a separate counteroffer form containing the changes. The counteroffer would then be presented to the buyer for acceptance.

Here, "acceptance" by the seller of the buyer's offer was not an acceptance at all. The alterations written on the buyer's offer constituted a *rejection* of the offer, by way of a counteroffer using an improper technique called *change-and-initial*.

The counteroffer creates a new offer that good brokerage practice requires be presented on a separate form. By using a separate counteroffer form, the broker promotes clarity for interpreting the contract should a dispute arise. More importantly, the defacing of a signed document has been avoided. [See **first tuesday** Form 180 accompanying this chapter]

The "change-and-initial" method of creating a counteroffer often leaves uncertainty as to when and who placed which terms in the contract. Also, the contract will be interpreted against the individual creating the uncertainty, typically the seller who countered by first defacing and then initialing a signed original document — all with the broker's unethical assistance. [CC §1654]

Analyzing the counteroffer form

A counteroffer may be made when the offer submitted is not acceptable and must be rejected or allowed to expire unaccepted.

A *rejection* can occur by a written rejection which states no counteroffer will be forth-

coming, or by submitting an alternative offer, called a *counteroffer*. After a rejection, the original offer can no longer be accepted to automatically form a binding agreement. [See **first tuesday** Form 184]

A rejection by presenting a counteroffer occurs in one of two ways:

1. An incorporation in a new offer of all the terms in the offer submitted which are then modified by alternative or additional provisions entered on the counteroffer form.

   or

2. A preparation of an entirely new offer on a fresh purchase agreement form (or exchange form, etc.) which is then submitted as a counteroffer.

The counteroffer form has four sections, each with a separate purpose explained as follows:

1. *Reference to prior offer*: The purpose of a counteroffer form is to reference a prior written offer and state the terms and conditions contrary to or in addition to those in the prior offer which are agreeable to the person making the counteroffer.

   Thus, the prior offer is identified by the type of agreement it is, its date and the property in question.

2. *The agreement offered:* The offer submitted and rejected by a counteroffer has all its terms and conditions "incorporated" into the counteroffer. Terms which are additional to or in conflict with those of the prior offer are then entered on the counteroffer form to create the terms and conditions of the new offer. Any terms in conflict with the terms of the prior offer override and become the terms of the counteroffer.

COUNTEROFFER

DATE:_____, 20_____, at _____, California

Items left blank or unchecked are not applicable.

FACTS:

1. This is a counteroffer to the following:
   - ☐ Purchase agreement
   - ☐ Exchange agreement
   - ☐ Counteroffer
   - ☐ Other:_____

   1.1 Dated:_____, 20_____, at _____, California

   1.2 Agreed to by: _____

   1.3 Regarding real estate referred to as: _____

   _____

AGREEMENT:

2. The undersigned includes all the terms and conditions of the above referred agreement in this counteroffer SUBJECT TO the following modifications:

   _____

   _____

   _____

   _____

   _____

   _____

   _____

   _____

   _____

3. This Counteroffer will be deemed revoked unless accepted in writing and delivered to the undersigned or their broker prior to the time of _____.m. on _____, 20_____.

BUYER'S BROKER: _____	SELLER'S BROKER:_____
Agent: _____	Agent:_____
Address: _____	Address: _____
_____	_____
Phone: _____	Phone: _____
I agree to purchase this property as stated above.	**I agree to sell this property as stated above.**
Date:_____, 20_____	Date:_____, 20_____
Buyer: _____	Seller: _____
Buyer: _____	Seller: _____
Address: _____	Address: _____
_____	_____
Phone: _____	Phone: _____
Fax: _____	Fax: _____

FORM 180   10-00   ©2004 first tuesday, P.O. BOX 20069 RIVERSIDE, CA 92516 (800) 794-0494

3. *Time for acceptance*: The counteroffer expires at the time and on the date stated for expiration. If no specific date is given, a reasonable time to accept is permitted, unless the counteroffer is first withdrawn.

4. *Signatures*: The party making the counteroffer signs and dates the offer. The brokers sign the counteroffer only to acknowledge their participation in the negotiations since they are not parties to the offer or its acceptance.

Preparing the counteroffer

Identification: Enter the date and the place the counteroffer is prepared. This is the date used to reference the counteroffer.

Facts:

1. *Prior offer*: **Check** the box that identifies the type of agreement which was submitted and rejected by the counteroffer.

    1.1 *Identification date of prior offer*: **Enter** the identification date from the submitted offer which is being countered.

    1.2 *Maker of prior offer*: **Enter** the name of the party who made the offer that will be terminated by the counteroffer.

    1.3 *Property identification*: **Enter** the legal, common description or assessor's parcel number of the property involved in the transaction.

Agreement:

2. *Counteroffer to terms and conditions*: This clause accepts all terms of the prior offer or counteroffer, subject to the modifications desired.

Enter the additional and alternative terms desired. When signed and submitted, the counteroffer constitutes a rejection of the referenced offer and is a new offer on an alternative set of terms.

CAUTION: Some purchase agreements fail to include the brokerage fee in the terms of the offer. When the brokerage fee is set out beneath the buyer's signature in an offer, include the brokerage fee in the counteroffer and do not sign the acceptance provision of the original offer — it has been rejected. **first tuesday's** forms include the brokerage fee in the buyer's offer, so any counteroffer referencing the prior offer automatically includes the brokerage fee.

3. *Time for acceptance*: **Enter** the date and time period for expiration of the counteroffer.

Signatures:

Buyer's broker identification: **Enter** the name of the buyer's broker, address, telephone number and the agent acting on the broker's behalf.

Seller's broker identification: **Enter** the name of the seller's broker, address, telephone number and the agent acting on the broker's behalf.

Buyer's signature: **Enter** the date, name, address, telephone number and fax number of the buyer. Obtain the buyer's signature.

Seller's signature: **Enter** the date, name, address, telephone number and fax number of the seller. Obtain the seller's signature.

Chapter 3

Property related disclosures

This chapter reviews a broker's use of unverified information when marketing real estate.

Sold "as-is" is a prohibited disclaimer — sell property "as-disclosed"

A broker and his sales agents must disclose the physical nature and condition of a property when soliciting an offer to purchase.

Brokers and agents have a duty to *timely disclose* to all parties involved in a real estate transaction any significant physical aspects of a property that may affect the property's market value.

To comply with this duty, the listing broker (or seller) of a one-to-four unit residence must provide the buyer with a Transfer Disclosure Statement (TDS) prior to making an offer and disclose all defects then known to the broker or the seller. [Calif. Civil Code §1102 et seq; See **first tuesday** Form 304]

To be effective, property disclosures must be made to the buyer before offers are prepared and prices agreed to. If not, the buyer may:

1. Cancel on discovery of the broker's failure to previously disclose.

   or

2. Close escrow and seek recovery of the costs to cure the belatedly disclosed and previously known defects, unless a contingency exists in the purchase agreement for further approval of the property's condition.

Any attempt to have the buyer waive his right to the mandated property disclosure statement is unenforceable. Failure to disclose property conditions is against public policy. [CC §1102]

The seller of one-to-four unit residential property must always prepare and deliver a Transfer Disclosure Statement (TDS). [See **first tuesday** Form 304]

Further, a broker has a general duty to all parties in any type of sales transaction to disclose at the earliest possible moment his awarness of any property defects.

For example, a seller's listing broker is aware the residence fails to conform to building and zoning regulations, a defect which if known to a buyer might affect the price he is willing to pay — a material fact.

The broker knows the buyer who is interested in making an offer is not aware of the violations and might reconsider the price he is willing to pay for the property if he learns of the violations. The broker decides not to disclose his knowledge of the defect.

In an attempt to cover the omission, the broker writes an "as-is" disclaimer provision into the purchase agreement, stating the buyer accepts the property in an as-is condition and has satisfied himself as to the property's conditions.

After the buyer acquires the property, the city refuses to provide utility services to the residence due to the building and zoning violations.

The buyer demands his money losses from the broker, claiming the broker breached his agency duty to disclose conditions of the property known to the broker.

The broker claims the buyer waived his right to collect money damages when he signed the purchase agreement with the "as-is" disclaimer (as is done with car sales).

Does an "as-is" disclaimer shield the broker from liability for the buyer's losses caused by the building and zoning violations?

No! The listing broker has a **general duty**, owed to all parties to a transaction, to disclose all property conditions that affect the value and marketability of the property which, due to an inspection, were or should have been known to the broker. This duty is not excused by writing an "as-is" disclaimer into the purchase agreement in lieu of making the factual disclosures. [**Katz** v. **Department of Real Estate** (1979) 96 CA3d 895]

Finally, public policy prohibits the sale of one-to-four unit residential property "as-is," causing most form publishers to eliminate boilerplate "as-is" clauses." [CC §1102.1]

Real estate size and boundaries must be accurately represented

Consider a broker who is the exclusive agent of a buyer in the purchase of a one-to-four unit residential property. Without first receiving a survey or title report to verify his representations, the broker advises the buyer about the amount of acreage and the extent of an easement on the property. A further-approval contingency calling for the buyer to confirm the representations is not included in the purchase agreement. The buyer purchases the property, relying on the broker's size and easement representations of the property.

More than two years after closing, the buyer discovers the acreage and easement representations made by the broker are false. The property is worth less than the price paid.

The buyer seeks to recover the difference in property value from the broker. The broker claims the buyer's recovery is barred by a two-year statute of limitations for breach of a broker's agency duty to **inspect and disclose** defects on one-to-four unit residential property.

The buyer claims his action is not time-barred since the two-year statute of limitations only applies to *negligent misrepresentations*, not to the recovery of a loss caused by the broker's intentional misrepresentations about facts related to the property's physical condition.

Here, the buyer is entitled to recover his loss in property value. The broker misrepresented the property's size and easement without first confirming what they consisted of, an intentional misrepresentation. The two-year statute of limitation only applies to a broker who inspects the property and, as a result of the inspection, *negligently fails* to disclose facts that a reasonably diligent on-site inspection would have revealed.

Here, the broker made representations *as fact* without first verifying the information or advising the buyer of his source of information and that the information was not verified. Thus, a three-year statute of limitations for intentional misrepresentation applies, commencing on the date the buyer discovers the falsity of the broker's representation. [**Field** v. **Century 21 Klowden-Forness Realty** (1998) 63 CA4th 18]

Now consider a broker who markets real estate through a Multiple Listing Service (MLS) publication. The property's square footage is listed in the MLS publication as an approximation based on unverified information. The broker conducts a visual inspection of the property.

A buyer enters into a purchase agreement for a price based on the square footage printed in the MLS publication. The purchase agreement includes a *disclaimer* that states the MLS marketing information is an approximation and advises the buyer to obtain an appraisal of the property. A further-approval contingency provision is not included allowing the buyer to confirm the disclosure or cancel the transaction.

The buyer closes escrow without first obtaining an appraisal of the property as advised. Later, the buyer discovers the property has significantly less square footage than approximated in the MLS marketing information. The price paid for the property exceeded the value received.

The buyer seeks to recover his lost property value from the broker, claiming the broker should have known based on his visual inspection that the square footage listed in the MLS markerting information was an exaggeration, not an approximation.

The broker claims he is not liable for the buyer's reduction in property value since the buyer has a responsibility to determine the exact square footage and property value before closing as advised in the purchase agreement.

However, the broker is responsible for the difference in property value due to the broker's misrepresentation of the square footage that was stated as an approximation in the MLS marketing information. The broker **should have known** his repre-

sentation of the square footage was an exaggeration which would be relied on by a buyer to set the price for the property. [**Furla** v. **Jon Douglas Company** (1998) 65 CA4th 1069]

Further, buyers and sellers have no duty to comply with a broker's advisory disclaimer. A contingency to be satisfied by an appraisal should have been provided, not a disclaimer.

Knowingly misrepresenting potential use

A broker and his agents must accurately represent the title restrictions (CC&Rs) and potential use (zoning) of real estate to a prospective buyer or tenant.

For example, a seller's residence has a detached garage which has been converted into an apartment. The seller lists his property for sale with a broker.

The seller built and rents out the apartment in violation of zoning ordinances. The broker does not visually inspect the property to assure himself the apartment is up to building code nor does he confirm that the rental activities comply with zoning ordinances known to him.

The broker induces a buyer to pay a higher price than the residence alone is worth, representing as an incentive the existence of rental income from the apartment. The purchase agreement does not contain a further-approval contingency to confirm that the rental income will be available, and if not, to cancel the agreement.

After escrow closes, the city notifies the buyer the garage apartment is being rented in violation of zoning ordinances. The buyer is forced to quit renting out the apartment, suffering a loss in value of the property.

Here, the broker is liable for the part of the purchase price the buyer paid in excess of the fair market value of the residence. The broker failed to determine the accuracy of his rental income disclosure by first determining whether zoning conditions limited the buyer's use of the property. [**Barder** v. **McClung** (1949) 93 CA2d 692]

In another example, an owner contacts a broker to arrange an exchange of his property for other real estate he seeks to purchase.

The broker locates replacement property, but does not disclose his knowledge that the second trust deed encumbering the replacement property contains a due-on-sale clause that allows the trust deed loan to be called due and payable after the closing of a sale.

The owner agrees to take title to the replacement property subject to the existing second trust deed. No contingency existed to provide for the further approval of a beneficiary statement and trust deed conditions or cancellation of the agreement.

After escrow closes, the second trust deed lender discovers the transfer to the owner and calls the loan under the due-on-sale clause.

The owner fails to pay the loan balance that is now due on the second. Ultimately, the owner loses the property at the second trust deed lender's foreclosure sale.

Here, the broker is liable for the owner's loss of equity due to the foreclosure. The broker failed to disclose his knowledge about the existence and legal consequences of the due-on-sale clause in the second trust deed taken over by the owner. The broker's

liability is the value of the equity lost in the replacement property as established by the price set by the broker in the exchange agreement, not the (lesser) fair market (cash) value of the property. [**Pepitone** v. **Russo** (1976) 64 CA3d 685]

The due-on-sale clause is a title condition that may affect a buyer's ability to retain ownership and use of the property.

The broker, marketing property other than a one-to-four unit residential property, must determine and disclose to the buyer any use restrictions on the property (e.g., zoning ordinances, easements, CC&Rs, title conditions) which may interfere with the buyer's intended use as disclosed to the broker.

Additionally, the broker's duty to disclose a known potential future use of the property extends beyond disclosure of title and zoning conditions and their affect on the future use of property.

For example, a buyer is interested in purchasing undeveloped property for commercial development.

The property is located next to a maintenance yard owned by the state.

The seller's broker has been previously contacted by the state regarding its intent to acquire the property to expand the maintenance yard when funds for the acquisition become available.

During purchase negotiations, the buyer asks the seller's broker if the state is interested in the property. The broker informs the buyer the state has no interest in acquiring the property.

The buyer enters into a purchase agreement with the seller. During escrow, the buyer has plans drawn and obtains the necessary permits for development and construction on the property.

Just before escrow closes, the buyer discovers the state intends to acquire the property — by condemnation if necessary.

The buyer proceeds to take title to the property and later grants the property to the state in a condemnation proceeding.

Here, the broker is liable for the out-of-pocket losses incurred by the buyer for his loss of use of the property, as well as punitive damages for the broker's intentional failure to disclose the state's interest in acquiring the property. The buyer relied on the broker's information regarding the state's activities when he determined whether the property was suitable for his future development plans. [**People** v. **Grocers Wholesale Co.** (1989) 214 CA3d 498]

Consider a buyer who makes an offer to purchase a residence. The broker is aware of a large structural crack in the foundation of the residence that is not apparent on a visual inspection. The broker delivers a "clean" condition of property statement (TDS) to the buyer stating the residence has no defective conditions. [See **first tuesday** Form 304]

More than two years later, the buyer discovers the crack. The buyer claims the broker is liable for the cost of repairing the foundation since he knew of and failed to disclose the crack in the foundation. The broker claims the buyer's action is barred by the two-year statute of limitations for misrepresentation since he only owed the buyer the statutory duty to disclose defects which would be revealed by a visual inspection.

Is the broker liable to the buyer for intentionally misrepresenting the existence of the crack in spite of the two-year statute of limitations for negligent misrepresentations?

Yes! The buyer's claim is not time-barred under statutes requiring the broker to visually inspect and disclose observable defective property conditions. Liability is imposed on the broker for his intentional misrepresentation, by omission, of his actual knowledge of the condition of the property when he stated defective conditions did not exist on the property when he knew they did. [**Williams** v. **Bennet Realtors** (1997) 52 CA4th 857]

Marketability disclosure

A broker and his agents must advise a prospective buyer or tenant of any known facts that will affect the value or desirability of the purchased or rented property.

Four categories of conditions contribute to or detract from the value of property:

1. Physical condition of soil and improvements.

2. Land use and title conditions.

3. Operating income and expenses.

4. Location hazards and surrounding area impact.

For example, a buyer seeks property for the purpose of increasing his personal income and wealth.

A broker recommends an apartment complex as the source of additional spendable income and equity buildup for the buyer.

The property's scheduled rental income is represented to be far greater than the actual income. Additionally, the broker contends the property is in excellent physical condition with no deferred maintenance. It is not.

The broker makes these representations based on information received from the seller. The broker does not investigate maintenance, expense, and income records of the property to check the accuracy of the seller's representations. More importantly, the broker does not advise the buyer that the seller is the source of the property information and that he has not confirmed the information.

At the urging of the seller, the buyer is dissuaded from inspecting the property by the broker.

Relying solely on the broker's representations as to the operating income and condition of the property, the buyer purchases the property.

After closing, the buyer realizes the operating income is far less than the scheduled income stated on the property operating statement. The buyer discovers tenants are delinquent in the payment of rent and incurs deferred maintenance expenses — all of which seriously reduce the projected net spendable income.

Eventually, the buyer defaults on his trust deed and loses the property in foreclosure.

A broker marketing property as an income-producing investment owes a duty to a buyer to research whether the property produces adequate income to meet expenses. Alternatively, the broker may include a contingency provision in the purchase agreement calling for the buyer to confirm the representations or cancel the agreement prior to closing.

The broker cannot merely pass on the statements made by the seller as to the property's condition and income and expenses generated by the property. The broker must advise the buyer about the source of the information and the need for further investigation. Thus, the broker is liable to the buyer for the buyer's lost property value. [**Ford** v. **Cournale** (1973) 36 CA3d 172]

A broker analyzes the suitability of income property by preparing or having the seller prepare an Annual Property Operating Data Sheet (APOD) and reviewing it with the buyer. [See **first tuesday** Form 352]

A completed APOD should be prepared when listing income property and attached to the listing agreement as an addendum signed by the seller.

In addition to income and expense information provided in the APOD, the broker should inspect the property for quality of income, deferred maintenance and desirability of location, as well as check for any title or zoning conditions which might interfere with the buyer's intended use of the property.

Another fact affecting the value and desirability of the property is the existence of due-on-sale clauses in new or existing trust deeds and whether the lender will call or recast the loan by adjusting rates and rescheduling payments.

A broker has a duty to investigate the accuracy of all representations he makes to buyers or lenders regarding a property's physical condition, use and operating expenses, unless he discloses the source of his information and the fact he has not investigated or confirmed the representations.

However, a broker of one-to-four unit residential property is relieved of the responsibility of verifying the representations regarding property conditions he receives from others and passes on to buyers as long as the source of information is disclosed to the buyer. The source typically is the seller, the seller's broker or a home inspector. [CC §§2079 et seq.]

For example, a seller's broker hands a buyer of one-to-four unit residential property a condition of property statement signed by the seller. The statement includes an additional comment by the broker on observable cracks in the walls, noting the **seller identified** them as cosmetic. The broker does not know they are not just cosmetic.

After closing, the buyer of the property incurs repair costs due to unstable soil. The buyer claims the seller's broker is liable for the costs since he failed to independently verify the seller's claims regarding the cracks in the walls. The broker claims he is not liable since he had no duty to verify the seller's representations of property conditions unknown to him.

Here, the broker is not liable for the buyer's losses. The broker only has a duty to inspect and disclose material facts **observable or known** to him, not to independently verify the claims of his disclosed source. [**Robinson** v. **Grossman** (1997) 57 CA4th 634]

Public record investigations

Now, consider a buyer who purchases a unit in a common interest development (CID) after receiving literature about the unit's fair market value and the development's potential for appreciation in value. The seller of the property does not disclose to the brokers or the buyer the existence of pending litigation between the homeowner's association (HOA) and the developer of the CID regarding soil subsidence in the common area.

Both the buyer's broker and the seller's broker conduct visual inspections of the property. Neither broker discovers any visible defects nor are any defects known to either of them.

After purchasing the property, the buyer learns of the litigation and the soil subsidence in the common areas. The buyer claims the brokers' failure to discover and disclose the pending litigation and the reasons for it is a breach of their statutory duty to investigate and disclose the condition and marketability of the property. The brokers claim they did not breach their duty to investigate and disclose since they were unaware of both the pending litigation and the soil subsidence.

Are the brokers responsible for their failure to investigate the records and disclose these material facts to the buyer?

No! The brokers of a one-to-four unit sale have no duty to investigate *public records* and disclose any pending litigation or soil subsidence not known to them. Further, the brokers were unaware of the existence of either the litigation or the soil subsidence. While a broker has a duty to investigate and confirm all representations he makes about a property or provide for the buyer to do so, the broker is not held accountable for representations by sellers which are outside his realm of knowledge. [**Padgett** v. **Phariss** (1997) 54 CA4th 1270]

Disclosures by interim title holders

Now consider a broker who acts as a relocation agent. The broker purchases the seller's one-to-four unit residence and later resells the property to a buyer, as anticipated by himself and the seller.

The broker hands the buyer the seller's condition of property disclosure which the broker received from the seller. In it, the seller does not disclose the existence of noise conditions in the surrounding area that affect the property's value. The broker is not aware of the noise conditions and does not add them to the disclosure statement.

On occupying the property, the buyer discovers the undisclosed noise conditions. As a result of the noise, the value of the property is less than the price paid.

The buyer seeks to recover the lost value from the broker who sold him the property. The broker claims he is not obligated to the buyer for the lost value since he was unaware of any noise conditions. The buyer claims the broker is liable for the lost value since he has a duty to investigate and verify the representations made by the seller on the condition of property statement.

Here, the broker is not liable to the buyer for the lost value resulting from undisclosed noise in the area surrounding the property. The existence of the condition was outside the realm of the broker's knowledge. [**Shapiro** v. **Sutherland** (1998) 64 CA4th 1534]

Now consider a buyer's broker who hands his prospective buyer of a unit in a residential condominium project (CID) a copy of the HOA's letter. The letter reviews the HOA's lawsuit against the developer regarding water intrusion in the condominium complex. The broker advises the buyer he has no further knowledge about the litigation and has not conducted an investigation into the background or status of the lawsuit.

After purchasing the property, the buyer discovers water intrusion in his unit that was not noticeable on prior inspections. The buyer claims the broker breached his agency duty to investigate and disclose the existence of the defects since the broker failed to verify the contents of the letter and provide him with a copy of the lawsuit.

However, a buyer's broker does not have a duty to investigate or deliver documents to the buyer concerning *public records* if the buyer knows his broker is merely passing on unverified information he received from others. [**Pagano** v. **Krohn** (1997) 60 CA4th 1]

Chapter 4

The borrower and loan broker relationship

This chapter explores the relationship between a borrower and loan broker.

Inducing a borrower to employ a broker

A broker or sales agent may not induce a borrower of a real estate loan or a seller of a trust deed note to retain the services of the broker by representing the existence of a lender or investor willing to make the loan or purchase the trust deed note when one does not exist.

For example, a real estate owner contacts a broker who arranges trust deed loans.

The owner informs the broker of the loan terms he will accept and asks the broker if he knows of a lender willing to make such a loan.

The broker does not now know of a lender who would be willing to make the loan sought by the owner, but believes he can locate one.

However, to persuade the owner to employ him, the broker assures the owner he knows of lenders who will make this type of loan. The owner is advised the broker will proceed to arrange the loan with one of these lenders if he will enter into a loan broker listing with the broker. [See **first tuesday** Form 104 accompanying this chapter]

Relying on the broker's representation that a lender exists who is willing to make the loan, the owner signs the listing.

The broker's attempts to locate a lender are unsuccessful.

The owner later discovers the broker never knew of a real estate lender who would originate a loan on the borrower's terms.

The owner files a complaint with the Department of Real Estate (DRE). The owner claims the broker had a duty to honestly represent the fact that no lenders existed at the time he employed the broker.

The broker's false claim that a lender existed who made the type of loan the owner was seeking is cause for the DRE to revoke or suspend the broker's license. [Calif. Business and Professions Code §10177(d)]

Also, the broker could be fined up to $10,000 or imprisoned up to six months — or both. [B & P C §10185]

No "free services" under a listing

A broker may not represent a specific service he provides for a client as "free" when he knows he will be compensated for that service advertised as free by charging a fee on the entire transaction.

For example, a broker wants to induce a seller of real estate to enter into an exclusive right-to-sell listing.

The broker offers "free advertising" of the seller's real estate, without any charge to the seller. Believing the advertising incentive is an extra service, the seller enters into an exclusive listing agreement with the broker.

However, a seller's broker is duty bound to advertise the seller's property no matter who pays the advertising costs. Advertising is part of the diligence required of a broker to market the property under an exclusive right-to-sell listing.

The broker, by use of the "free advertising" gimmick, has represented as free an activity that a diligent broker is **required to provide** for a client. The advertised activity is not free, but offered in expectation of compensation under the listing. [**Coleman** v. **Mora** (1968) 263 CA2d 137]

The broker's bargain under an exclusive listing agreement consists of fulfilling one essential duty — the diligent pursuit of his client's real estate goals.

Also, the broker must take reasonable steps to gather and analyze all facts concerning the physical condition of the property, its title conditions, operating data and location.

The broker must evaluate and disclose to his client the information he has gathered about the property.

The broker performs numerous activities while exercising diligence and advising his client about the implications of a transaction, including the financial, legal, tax and risk aspects the client might encounter in the transaction. The broker is compensated for his diligence under the listing agreement.

Thus, the broker cannot represent as "free of charge" a brokerage activity he must perform as a matter of being diligent in a transaction on which he is paid a fee.

Advance fees must be accounted for before disbursement

A broker arranging a real estate loan as the agent for a borrower must account to the borrower for any advance fees received prior to the disbursement of the loan funds.

Editor's note — An advance fee is a fee received by a broker for soliciting borrowers or lenders to arrange or sell real estate loans before brokerage services are performed. The rule also applies to real estate sales transactions. [B & P C §10026]

However, advance fees must be distinguished from advance costs!

Advance costs are deposits handed to the broker to cover out-of-pocket costs incurred on behalf of the depositor while performing brokerage services, such as a loan appraisal for a borrower or ordering termite work done for a seller.

For example, a borrower seeking to purchase nonresidential real estate employs a broker who agrees to help him obtain a loan for a fee.

The broker tells the borrower the fee must be paid in advance as compensation for his initial time spent in preparing the loan package and negotiating with the lender.

The borrower writes a check to the broker for $1,000, indicating on the check the money is an advance fee for services to be rendered in preparing and arranging the loan.

Instead of depositing the check into a trust fund account, the broker deposits the client's money into his general business account. The broker believes the funds are his to spend as he sees fit.

Later, the borrower, having received no billing or accounting, demands an accounting of the funds. The broker is unable (or unwilling) to provide the borrower with any documentation as to what services were rendered, how much time was spent or when and to whom the funds were disbursed.

LOAN BROKERING LISTING
Exclusive Right to Borrow

DATE:_____, 20_____, at _____, California

Items left blank or unchecked are not applicable.

1. **RETAINER COMMITMENTS:**

    1.1 Owner hereby retains and grants to Broker the exclusive right to locate a lender and arrange a loan to be secured by the property described herein, for the period:
    beginning on _____, 20_____ and terminating on _____, 20_____.

    1.2 Broker to use diligence in the performance of this employment. Owner to cooperate with broker to meet the objectives of this employment.

    1.3 Owner hands $_____ to Broker for deposit into Broker's trust account for application to Owner's obligations under this agreement and the following attachments:

       a. ☐ Advance Fee Addendum [**first tuesday** Form 106]

       b. ☐ Listing Package Cost sheet [**ft** Form 107]

2. **ADDENDUMS to this agreement:**

    a. ☐ Credit Application [**ft** Form 302]

    b. ☐ Borrower's Loan Disclosure [**ft** Form 325]

    c. ☐ Condition of Property (Transfer) Disclosure [**ft** Form 304]

    d. ☐ APOD (Annual Property Operating Data) [**ft** Form 352 or **ft** Form 562 for a SFR]

    e. ☐ Rental Income Statement [**ft** From 380]

    f. ☐ Refinance Cost Sheet [**ft** Form 312]

    g. ☐ See Addendum for additional provisions [**ft** Form 250]

    h. ☐ _____

    i. ☐ _____

3. **BROKERAGE FEE:**

    NOTICE: The amount or rate of real estate fees is not fixed by law. They are set by each Broker individually and may be negotiable between the Client and Broker.

    3.1 Owner agrees to pay Broker _____ of the principal amount of the loan sought or obtained, IF:

       a. Anyone procures a lender on the terms stated in this agreement, or any other terms acceptable to Owner, during the period of this agreement.

       b. The property is withdrawn as collateral, or title is made unmarketable as collateral by Owner during the retainer period.

       c. The Owner terminates this employment of the Broker during the retainer period.

       d. Within one year after termination of this agreement, the Owner or his agent commences negotiations which later result in a transaction contemplated by this agreement with a lender with whom the Broker, or a cooperating broker, negotiated during the period of this agreement. Broker to identify prospective lenders by written notice to the owner within 21 days after termination of this agreement.

    3.2 Should this agreement terminate without Owner becoming obligated to pay Broker a fee, Owner to pay Broker the sum of $_____ per hour of time accounted for by Broker, not to exceed $_____.

4. LOAN TERMS:

4.1 Loan sought is $_____, payable as follows:

a. Interest at an annual rate of no more than _____%, ☐ fixed, ☐ ARM type _____.

b. Payments due ☐ monthly, or ☐ _____, amortized over _____ years.

c. Final/balloon payment due _____, 20_____.

d. Late charge: _____

e. Prepayment penalty: _____

f. Loan escrow with _____

g. A lender's ALTA policy purchased by Owner in the amount of the loan.

Title Company: _____

5. REAL ESTATE SECURING THE LOAN:

5.1 Type: _____

Address: _____

Described as: _____

_____

Vesting: _____

5.2 The priority for the lien securing the loan sought will be ☐ first, or ☐ second.

5.3 Encumbrances of record:

a. A first loan in the amount of $_____ payable $_____ per month until paid, including interest at _____%, ☐ ARM type _____, due _____, 20_____, impounds being $_____ monthly.

Lender: _____

b. A second loan in the amount of $_____ payable $_____ per month, including interest at _____%, due_____, 20_____.

Lender: _____

c. Other encumbrance, bond, assessment or lien in the amount of $_____.

Lienholder: _____

5.4 My purchase price on _____ was $_____.

Since the purchase of the property, I have invested in repairs and improvements approximately $_____.

5.5 The current fair market value is $_____.

Property taxes for the year 20_____ were $_____.

5.6 The property is occupied by _____

at a rental rate of $_____ per month, under a:

☐ rental agreement; or

☐ lease agreement which expires _____, 20_____.

a. ☐ See attached Rental Income Statement. [ft Form 380]

_____

_____

_____

6. **PERSONAL PROPERTY INCLUDED AS COLLATERAL:**

   6.1 Described as: _____

   _____

   _____

   _____

   _____

   6.2 Encumbered for the amount of $_____ payable $_____ monthly, including interest
   at _____%, due _____, 20_____.

   Lender: _____

7. **GENERAL PROVISIONS:**

   7.1 Broker is authorized to disclose, publish, discuss, and disseminate among prospective lenders the financial information supplied by Owner or credit agencies.

   7.2 Owner warrants all necessary permits have been obtained for any additions, alterations, repairs, installations or replacements to the structure or its components, except: _____.

   a. ☐ See attached Condition of Property (TDS). [ft Form 304]

   7.3 Owner authorizes Broker to cooperate with other agents and divide with them any compensation due.

   7.4 In any action to enforce this agreement, the prevailing party shall receive reasonable attorney fees.

   7.5 This listing agreement will be governed by California law.

   7.6 _____

   _____

   _____

   _____

   _____

   _____

   _____

   _____

   _____

   _____

I agree to render services on the terms stated above.	**I agree to employ Broker on the terms stated above.**
Date:_____, 20_____	Date:_____, 20_____
Broker's Name:_____	Owner's Name: _____
By: _____	Owner's Name: _____
Address: _____	Signature:_____
_____	Signature:_____
	Address:_____
Phone: _____	_____
	Phone: _____
Fax: _____	Fax: _____
E-mail: _____	E-mail: _____

FORM 104   10-01   ©2004 **first tuesday**, P.O. BOX 20069 RIVERSIDE, CA 92516 (800) 794-0494

Further, the broker cannot even prove the funds were spent on services rendered on the borrower's behalf.

The borrower employed the broker to obtain a loan and was requested to pay a fee in advance before the broker would render any services. Thus, the broker received a deposit for a fee he had not yet earned and failed to place the deposit into his trust account for disbursement after the fee was earned. The broker also failed to account for time spent working on the borrower's behalf before placing the funds in his general account. [**Nelson** v. **Department of Real Estate** (1984) 161 CA3d 939; B & P C §§10026; 10146]

Any fees received by the broker before services are performed must be deposited into the broker's trust account, separate from the broker's own funds. [B & P C §10145]

The broker must use a DRE-approved advance fee form or obtain DRE approval of the advance fee form used. [B & P C §10085; See **first tuesday** Form 106]

After depositing the funds into the trust account, the broker can make withdrawals from the deposit. However, a withdrawal can only be made to compensate the broker for the services he has rendered arranging the loan for the borrower. [B & P C §10146]

Further, the broker cannot withdraw funds from the trust account for fees he has earned until five days after he accounts to the borrower for the services he has performed arranging the loan. [B & PC §10146; See Chapter 2 of Trust Funds]

Also, the broker is required to make a full accounting to the borrower at least every calendar quarter (including services ren-dered, amounts disbursed, payees, dates, etc.) for the withdrawal and expenditure of any advance fees deposited in the trust account. [B & P C §10146]

A broker's failure to account to his client for advance fees paid for arranging a real estate loan may result in the suspension of his license. The broker is also exposed to liability to the borrower for treble the borrower's damages for misappropriation of trust funds. [**Burch** v. **Argus Properties, Inc.** (1979) 92 CA3d 128]

Accurately represent loan terms to the borrower

A real estate licensee must make a meaningful disclosure about the essential terms of a real estate loan when soliciting a borrower or arranging a loan with a lender.

For example, a real estate broker advertises he can arrange loans with a low monthly payment schedule. In fact, loans of this type are not available.

A borrower, seeking a loan with the low payment schedule advertised by the broker, retains the services of the broker to arrange such a loan.

The borrower asks specific questions of the broker concerning the interest rate, late charges, the balloon payment on final payoff and closing costs.

The broker tells the borrower the balloon payment will be "small" and misrepresents the interest rate and the day of the month on which late charges are incurred. The broker provides the borrower with "approxima-tions" of the closing costs that are signifi-cantly lower than the true closing costs.

The broker also fails to accurately disclose other important loan aspects, such as the monthly payments are interest only, rather than an amortized reduction of the principal, or that late charges are equal in amount to the monthly interest payment.

Further, the financial disclosure statement is lengthy and contains complex wording which is not understood by the borrower. Instead of reading the disclosure statement, the borrower relies on the broker's oral representations and signs the loan documents.

Due to the underestimated closing costs, the borrower incurs additional and unexpected expenses, such as high late charges, an early due date, monthly payment adjustments and prepayment penalties. The additional expenses of payments and refinancing ultimately create an excessive financial burden for the borrower.

Eventually, the borrower defaults on the loan and loses the secured property through foreclosure.

Later, the borrower discovers the broker was aware of the actual loan terms and costs for origination when he agreed to the loan.

The broker's failure to disclose the actual interest rate, the exact amount of the late charge, the size of the balloon payment and the actual closing costs is a breach of his agency duty to his client, the borrower.

The borrower can recover all his money losses caused by the broker's misrepresentation of the terms of the loan and for failing to discuss important provisions in the loan documents with his client. [**Wyatt** v. **Union Mortgage Company** (1979) 24 C3d 773]

As the borrower's broker arranging a loan, a licensee must fully and accurately disclose all essential facts of the loan transaction which might affect the borrower's decision to participate in the transaction. [B & P C §§10130; 10131(d); 10176(a),(i)]

The licensee's duty to disclose and his obligation to deal fairly with borrowers commences on his first contact with prospective borrowers to solicit employment, before entering into a listing agreement or loan. [**Realty Projects Inc.** v. **Smith** (1973) 32 CA3d 204]

A prospective borrower has a right to expect a broker to accurately represent the terms of the loan offered, as well as give accurate estimates regarding loan costs, brokerage fees and escrow expenses.

Even after the broker is employed as the agent of the borrower, his duty of disclosure and accurate representation is not completed by merely providing the loan documents to the borrower. The provisions in the documents must be discussed with the client to ensure the client has an understanding sufficient to make a well-informed decision regarding his participation in the loan transaction. [B & P C §10241]

Chapter 5

The private lender and the loan broker

This chapter discusses the relationship between the private lender and the loan broker.

Use of the lender disclosure statement

A broker arranging a loan with a private lender must disclose the **priority** of the lender's trust deed relative to other liens against the real estate.

However, if a loan is arranged with an institutional lender, the broker need not provide the institutional lender with a lender's disclosure statement. [Calif. Business and Professions Code §10232.4(b); See **first tuesday** Form 326]

Also, if a loan is made by a broker while acting as both the lender (principal) and as an agent for the buyer or seller in a real estate sale, no disclosure statement to the lender-broker is required, as he would merely be advising himself. [B & P C §10230]

Consider a broker who completes a **lender's disclosure statement** with loan information received from a borrower (e.g., value of the property securing the loan, credit and financial information about the borrower, etc.). The statement is presented to prospective private lenders. [See **first tuesday** Form 326]

Each lender's disclosure statement also states whether the lender's trust deed will be junior to existing first and second trust deeds on the borrower's real estate.

Here, the broker has complied with his duty to disclose to prospective lenders all aspects of the proposed loan transaction, including the priority of each lender's trust deed relative to existing encumbrances on the real estate that will secure the loan. [B & P C §10232.4(a)]

In another example, an owner retains a broker to arrange two loans from separate lenders secured by the same property.

When negotiating the loans with different private lenders, the broker must disclose to each lender that the property will be encumbered by another trust deed lien not yet recorded. The priority of the respective new trust deed liens is to be disclosed in each lender's disclosure statement prepared by the broker. [B & P C §10232.5(a)(6)]

Disclose credit and financial information supplied on the borrower

A broker or sales agent negotiating the placement of a real estate loan or the sale of a trust deed note to a private lender or trust deed investor must disclose information about the prospective borrower's identity, occupation, employment, income and credit data as represented to the broker or sales agent by the prospective borrower. This is best accomplished through the use of a disclosure form. [See **first tuesday** Form 326]

For example, an owner of real estate contacts a loan broker to arrange a loan he needs.

An annual operating (income/expenses) statement and a net worth statement (balance sheet), called *financial statements*, are completed by the owner and handed to the broker.

The financial statements indicate to the broker that the owner has a moderate income, and does not have the ability to make payments on the loan sought.

Meanwhile, the broker requests and receives a credit report which indicates an excellent payment history and credit rating. However, when presenting his loan package to the lender, the broker fails to hand over the owner's financial statements or advise the lender the borrower has insufficient income to justify the loan amount and rate. The lender is informed only of the owner's "clean" credit history.

The lender makes the loan and the owner soon defaults due to insufficient income to cover his payment obligation.

However, a broker has a duty as a licensee to advise the lender, even if the lender is not his client, about the owner's income and expenses as disclosed by the owner or otherwise known to the broker, even though the owner's credit report indicates no past credit problems.

Before a lender decides to make a loan, information given by a borrower is used by the lender to objectively determine the future likelihood of the owner defaulting on the loan, and thus the risk undertaken and the interest rate, due date and security required to cover the risk of loss on a default.

A lender has a right to obtain sufficient facts from the borrower to make an informed decision on the risk of default it undertakes on making or allowing the assumption of the loan. [**Wellenkamp** v. **Bank of America** (1978) 21 C3d 943]

Private lenders rely on brokers to obtain information necessary to make a decision to lend based on the borrower's ability to comply with the terms of the loan. Private lenders frequently do not have the same resources as institutional lenders to determine the borrower's creditworthiness. Thus, private lenders employ brokers for the purpose of analyzing the risk of loss presented by the loan — and to pass on information received from the borrower and reporting agencies. [**Dawn Investment Co., Inc.** v. **Superior Court of Los Angeles County** (1982) 30 C3d 695]

The borrower's ability to repay

A broker or sales agent may not hand false or misleading information to real estate lenders and trust deed investors about a borrower's or owner's ability to repay a real estate loan.

For example, a buyer retains a broker to arrange a loan. As part of his loan package, the broker investigates the buyer's credit history through a credit reporting agency. The credit report informs the broker the buyer is inclined to make timely payments on his obligations.

Next, the broker analyzes information in financial statements provided by the buyer regarding his income, expenses and assets (operating and balance sheets).

Both the credit report and financial statements indicate a good credit rating and substantial income and assets.

The broker, attempting to verify information in the buyer's financial statements, discovers the buyer has significant additional expenses and loans he has not disclosed.

The broker has *reason to believe* the undisclosed expenses and loans will interfere with the buyer's ability to make his payments on the loan and increase the lender's risk of loss.

However, the broker does not tell the lender about the additional expenses and loans. Instead, the broker limits his disclosures to the buyer's good credit rating, high income, and substantial assets in the report produced by the buyer.

The lender makes the loan. Before the loan is repaid, the buyer declares bankruptcy and the lender suffers a loss on the loan.

The broker's failure to inform the lender about the buyer's undisclosed expenses and loans known to the broker, which if known to the lender might alter the lender's analysis of the loan, subjects the broker to discipline by the Department of Real Estate (DRE) on a complaint by the lender.

Also, the lender can recover his loan losses from the broker since the broker knew adverse credit information existed and intentionally omitted advising the lender about the significant adverse conditions, called *material facts*.

The borrower's loan history

A broker and his sales agents must disclose to real estate lenders and trust deed investors their knowledge of the borrower's:

- ability to make payments on the note; and
- propensity to maintain the property under the trust deed.

Disclosures regarding the borrower include the borrower's loan payment and property maintenance history and any delinquencies or defaults on the trust deed note being sold, and whether the borrower has a bankruptcy history.

For example, a borrower who owns a business retains a real estate broker to arrange a loan with a lender to be secured by the business, its inventory and his leasehold interest in the premises occupied by the business.

The broker investigates and analyzes the borrower's:

- credit history to determine the borrower's payment history;

- net worth to analyze the borrower's assets and liquidity; and

- income and expenses to calculate ratios on the borrower's capacity to pay.

Also, the broker contacts some of the borrower's past business associates for information on the borrower's management of his business and financial affairs, as well as care of the premises he occupied.

The broker discovers the borrower is currently in bankruptcy but will be released before the loan is originated. The pending bankruptcy is not included in the credit report.

The broker tells the lender only about the financial data obtained through the reports and statements. The pendency of the bankruptcy is not disclosed since the borrower will be released from bankruptcy prior to recording the new trust deed and it will not affect the title insurance for the loan.

The lender makes the loan which records after the release from bankruptcy. Later, the borrower reopens the bankruptcy and lists the new loan.

The lender claims he never would have made the loan to the borrower, or certainly would have charged a premium rate for the additional risk, had he known the borrower was, or had been within a few years, in bankruptcy when the loan was arranged.

Here, the broker was duty bound, as an agent in the loan transaction, to advise the lender of the borrower's pending bankruptcy while arranging the loan — even though the lender was not his client. The information is pertinent to an analysis of the borrower's ability to manage his affairs and the rate of interest to be charged to cover any additional risk of loss imposed on the lender by the borrower's level of care and management of his business.

Accurately disclose the condition and value of secured property

When soliciting a lender or arranging a real estate loan, a broker will accurately represent the market value, the physical condition and the size of the property securing the loan.

For example, a private lender retains a loan broker to arrange the investment of funds in second trust deed loans.

The loan broker hires an independent real estate appraiser to evaluate a property which is to secure a loan to be arranged for the private lender.

The appraiser submits an appraisal report on the property to the broker. The report states the value of the property to be much higher than the property's actual value.

The broker relies on the appraisal report and does not further investigate the property's value nor confirm the findings of the report.

The private lender agrees to make a loan secured by a second trust deed on the property based on its appraised value in the report obtained by the loan broker.

Later, the owner of the secured real estate defaults on the loan. The private lender's trust deed is wiped out when the first trust deed holder forecloses on the property. Recovery is not available under the now unsecured note due to the financial condition of the maker.

The private lender seeks to recover the loss of his investment from the loan broker because of the appraiser's misrepresentation of the value of the property.

The loan broker claims the private lender cannot hold him liable and must look to the appraiser for any recovery since the appraiser was an independent contractor retained by the loan broker.

Is the loan broker liable for the private lender's losses due to the appraiser's faulty appraisal of the property?

Yes! A loan broker has an agency duty to accurately represent the value of the property to the private lender.

A broker cannot delegate to an appraiser the duty to accurately ascertain the value of the property that will be or is the security for the loan. [**Barry** v. **Raskov** (1991) 232 CA3d 447]

The broker in *Barry* seeks to excuse himself of liability for the appraiser's faulty report on the property's value, claiming the issue of who caused the loss is between the appraiser and the lender.

However, the agency duty the broker owes to his principal, the private lender, to establish value cannot be *assigned to others* to avoid liability for any error in the performance of the duty owed. Further, the broker's responsibility for accurately advising the private lender about the value of the property which will secure the proposed loan cannot be shifted to others by use of disclaimers of responsibility, or advisory instructions to consult with other (more) professional advisors.

However, *indemnity* may be available to the broker to cover his liability if the broker acted in reliance on another individual's professional advice, such as an appraiser, certified public accountant (CPA), home inspector or attorney. [**Home Budget Loans, Inc.** v. **Jacoby and Meyers Law Offices** (1989) 207 CA3d 1277]

Also, a broker has the option of contracting for appraisal reports with an appraiser who carries errors and omissions insurance. Thus insured, the broker has a source of recovery under indemnification for the false information passed on to the client.

Further, the broker can monitor the appraiser's activities, with leverage over the appraiser's work through incentives such as repeat business and refusal to pay for unacceptable reports. [Barry, *supra*]

A broker's failure to accurately represent the value of property securing a loan subjects him to liability for money damages, and the possible suspension or revocation of his license by the DRE. [B & P C §§10176(a); 10177(g)]

Terms of loan originated or sold

The terms of a loan being originated or sold by a broker must be disclosed to the prospective private lender or individual trust deed investor in a lender's disclosure statement.

Loan terms include the amount of the loan, payment schedules, payoff provisions, and any lender/investor transactional costs. [See **first tuesday** Form 326]

Also, a broker selling a trust deed must include the payment terms of the trust deed investment in the disclosure statement handed to the investor. [B & PC §10232.5]

A broker arranging a loan must disclose in the statement to the lender any loan proceeds the broker will retain. [B & P C §10232.5(a)(9)]

Also, a broker arranging loans or selling trust deeds must account to the lender or investor for any loan payments he receives.

SECTION B

AGENCY

Chapter 1

Agency: authority to represent others

This chapter discusses the agency relationship between a real estate broker, his agents and his client.

Introduction to agency

Webster defines an agent as "a person...empowered to act for another." [Webster's New World Dictionary, Third College Edition (1988)]

Black's Law Dictionary describes agency as a "relation where one person acts for or represents another by the latter's authority..." [Black's Law Dictionary, Fifth Edition (1979]

The agency relationship can be as principal and agent, master and servant, or employer/proprietor and employee/independent contractor.

When the agency involves real estate as its subject matter, the California legislature has devised a **licensing scheme** to establish a minimum level of professional competency for licensing of individuals who act as agents in real estate related transactions.

A governmental agency, the Department of Real Estate (DRE), was created to oversee licensing and police a minimum level of competency for individuals desiring to represent others as real estate agents. Presently, this goal is pursued through the education of individuals who seek a license or are up for relicensing. The education is offered in the private and public sectors under government certification.

Agency in real estate related transactions includes relationships between:

- *brokers* and members of the public (clients or third parties);

- licensed *sales agents* and their brokers; and

- *finders* and their brokers or principals.

The **extent of representation** owed to a client by the broker and his agents depends on the *scope of authority* the client gives the broker, whether it is given orally, in writing or through the client's conduct with the broker. Also, minimum acceptable *standards of diligence* are set by the California legislature, the DRE and the courts.

Agency and representation are synonymous in real estate transactions. A broker, by accepting exclusive employment from a client, undertakes the task of aggressively using *due diligence* to represent the client and attain the objectives sought by the client. An open listing only imposes a *best efforts* standard of representation.

Real estate jargon

Real estate jargon used by brokers and sales agents tends to create confusion among members of the public. When the jargon is used in legislative schemes, it adds a high degree of statutory chaos, academic discussion and judicial and public consternation over the duties of the real estate licensee.

For example, the words **real estate agent**, as used in the brokerage industry, mean a *real estate salesperson employed by and representing a real estate broker*. Interestingly, real estate salespeople rarely refer to themselves as sales agents. Instead, they call themselves "realtors" or "broker associates."

Legally, however, a client's real estate agent is defined as a *real estate broker who undertakes representation of a client in a real estate transaction*. A salesperson is legally *an agent of the agent*.

The word "subagency" suffers from even greater contrasts. Subagency serves both as:

- jargon for fee-splitting agreements between Multiple Listing Service (MLS) member brokers; and

- a legal principle for the authorization given to one broker by another (listing) broker to also act as an agent on behalf of the listing broker's seller.

What is clear about real estate agency is the **primary duties** a broker and his agents owe the client, rather than the general duties owed to all parties regarding the real estate involved in the transaction. Primary duties owed a client, based on the best of the broker's knowledge, include:

- *evaluating* the financial impact of the proposed transaction on the client;

- *advising* on the legal consequences of documents which touch and affect the client in the proposed transaction;

- *considering* the tax aspects of the transfer, except in one-to-four unit residential sales; and

- *reviewing* the suitability of the client's exposure to a risk of loss on the transaction.

Clients can rescind all real estate contracts in a transaction when dual agency circumstances go undisclosed at the time of acceptance. The broker has misrepresented his agency to others in the transaction.

To protect both their clients and themselves, all real estate licensees must:

- *know* the scope of authority given to them by the employment agreement;

- *document* the agency tasks undertaken; and

- *possess* sufficient knowledge, determination and ability to perform the agency tasks they have undertaken.

In all tasks undertaken, a licensee must conduct himself at or above the minimum acceptable levels of competency to avoid liability to the client or disciplinary action by the DRE.

What is an agent?

An agent is an individual or corporation who **represents another**, called the *principal*, in dealings with third persons. Thus, a principal can never be his own agent since a principal acts for his own account, not on behalf of another.

The representation undertaken by a real estate broker is called an *agency*. Three parties are referred to in agency law: a principal, an agent and third persons. [Calif. Civil Code §2295]

In the brokerage of real estate transactions:

- the *agent* is the real estate broker retained to represent a client for the purposes hired;

- the *principal* is the client, such as a seller, buyer, landlord, tenant, lender or borrower who has retained a broker to sell, locate, lease or arrange a loan on real estate with other individuals; and

- *third persons* are individuals, or associations (corporations, limited partnerships and limited liability companies) other than the broker's client, with whom the broker has contact as an agent acting on behalf of his client.

Creation of the agency relationship

An agency relationship is created in a real estate transaction when a person, called the client or principal, employs and authorizes a broker, called the agent, to act on his behalf in the future. [CC §2307]

A broker's representation of a client, such as a buyer or seller, tenant or landlord, borrower or lender is properly undertaken and the fee agreement enforceable only after a written employment agreement has been signed by both the client and the broker. This employment contract is loosely referred to in the real estate industry as a "listing agreement." [**Phillippe** v. **Shapell Industries, Inc.** (1987) 43 C3d 1247]

The broker's agency can also be created by an oral agreement or conduct of the client with the broker or other individuals.

However, the fee arrangements would be unenforceable since no written agreement exists.

Also, some pre-printed, pre-1989 purchase agreements still in use contain a brokerage fee provision located below the signature of the buyer. The provision improperly stated the seller employs both the listing and selling brokers.

However, the intent of the brokers using the form is merely to split the fee being paid by the seller. This acceptance/fee provision becomes the seller's *employment* or *ratification* of the buyer's selling broker as an agent of the seller — even though the selling broker may never have acted on behalf of the seller, acting exclusively as the agent for the buyer.

This ill-conceived and combined acceptance/fee provision establishes the buyer's broker as the seller's subagent, or joint agent with the listing broker, a generally unacceptable legal consequence for the seller since representations to the buyer by the selling broker are binding on the seller. [**Johnston** v. **Seargeants** (1957) 152 CA2d 180]

These acceptance/fee provisions were finally altered to avoid imposing liability on the seller for representations made by the buyer's broker. The revision was necessary to avoid conflicts with the agency confirmation law enacted in the late 1980s for one-to-four unit residential sales.

Chapter 2

The agency law disclosure

This chapter examines the agency law disclosure and its timely presentation to sellers and buyers.

The industry's failures provoke legislation

In any established industry, such as real estate brokerage, rules and regulations exist to keep order and prevent chaos.

As an industry develops and matures, so does the need to keep the order running smoothly.

But when problems with professional conduct arise, and are overlooked or mishandled within the industry, sources from outside tend to feel compelled to step into the "power vacuum" created by the lack of internal order and take corrective action.

This lack of "self-policing" by the real estate industry prompted the enactment of an agency law disclosure by the California legislature.

The agency law disclosure is an attempt to cure a number of publicly misleading brokerage practices and establish uniform application of real estate terminology. The law is primarily a restatement of existing agency codes and the codification of case law. Additionally, the disclosure scheme made changes in the methods a broker must follow when disclosing agencies in one-to-four unit residential sales transactions.

Basically, an **agency law disclosure** form was created by the legislature to educate and familiarize clientele of brokers (as well as brokers and their agents) with:

- a uniform jargon for real estate transactions; and

- the various agency roles licensees undertake on behalf of their principals and other parties in a real estate related transaction.

Real estate brokers and their agents must, by use of the form, disclose to buyers and sellers, and long-term lessees and lessors, of one-to-four unit residential property the different agency relationships which may come into existence when working with a broker. The various agencies are made known to the seller and buyer by handing them the form since it contains a reprint of the entire statutory scheme for agency in real estate transactions.

The agency law disclosure is a two-page form, sometimes referred to as the *agency disclosure addendum*. It must be handed to a seller of one-to-four units on two occasions:

1. Before the seller employs the broker under a listing agreement.

2. On submission of a purchase agreement signed by the buyer. [See Form 305 accompanying this chapter]

In contrast, but also part of the same scheme, a separate **agency confirmation provision** is mandated for inclusion in purchase agreements. The agency confirmation provision in a purchase agreement advises the buyer and seller at the time they sign the purchase agreement of the agency relationship each broker has with each of them in the proposed transaction.

AGENCY LAW DISCLOSURE
Disclosure Regarding Real Estate Agency Relationships

DATE:_____, 20_____, at _____, California

To Seller/Buyer: _____

NOTICE: This agency disclosure complies with agency disclosures required with property listings and offers to buy, sell, exchange or lease one-to-four residential units and mobile homes. [Calif. Civil Code §2079 et seq.]

---

1. **FACTS:** When you enter into a discussion with a real estate agent regarding a real estate transaction, you should from the outset understand what type of agency relationship or representation you wish to have with the agent in the transaction.

2. **SELLER'S AGENT:** A Seller's agent under a listing agreement with the Seller acts as the agent for the Seller only. A Seller's agent or a subagent of that agent has the following affirmative obligations:
   - 2.1 To the Seller:
     - a. A fiduciary duty of utmost care, integrity, honesty and loyalty in dealings with the Seller.
   - 2.2 To the Buyer and the Seller:
     - a. Diligent exercise of reasonable skill and care in performance of the agent's duties.
     - b. A duty of honest and fair dealing and good faith.
     - c. A duty to disclose all facts known to the agent materially affecting the value of desirability of the property that are not known to, or within the diligent attention and observation of the parties.
   - 2.3 An agent is not obligated to reveal to either party any confidential information obtained from the other party which does not involve the affirmative duties set forth above.

3. **BUYER'S AGENT:** A selling agent can, with a Buyer's consent agree to act as agent for the Buyer only. In these situations, the agent is not the Seller's agent, even if by agreement the agent may receive compensation for services rendered, either in full or in part from the Seller. An agent acting only for a Buyer has the following affirmative obligations:
   - 3.1 To the Buyer:
     - a. A fiduciary duty of utmost care, integrity, honesty and loyalty in dealings with the Buyer.
   - 3.2 To the Buyer and the Seller:
     - a. Diligent exercise of reasonable skill and care in performance of the agent's duties.
     - b. A duty of honest and fair dealing and good faith.
     - c. A duty to disclose all facts known to the agent materially affecting the value or desirability of the property that are not known to, or within the diligent attention and observation of the parties. An agent is not obligated to reveal to either party any confidential information obtained from the other party which does not involve the affirmative duties set forth above.

4. **AGENT REPRESENTING BOTH SELLER AND BUYER:** A real estate agent, either acting directly or through one or more associate licensees, can legally be the agent of both the Seller and the Buyer in a transaction, but only with the knowledge and consent of both the Seller and the Buyer.
   - 4.1 In a dual agency situation, the agent has the following affirmative obligations to both the Seller and the Buyer:
     - a. A fiduciary duty of utmost care, integrity, honesty and loyalty in the dealings with either Seller or Buyer.
     - b. Other duties to the Seller and the Buyer as stated above in their respective sections.
   - 4.2 In representing both Seller and Buyer, the agent may not, without the express permission of the respective party, disclose to the other party that the Seller will accept a price less than the listing price or that the Buyer will pay a price greater than the price offered.

5. The above duties of the agent in a real estate transaction do not relieve a Seller or Buyer from the responsibility to protect their own interests. You should carefully read all agreements to assure that they adequately express your understanding of the transaction. A real estate agent is a person qualified to advise about real estate. If legal or tax advice is desired, consult a competent professional.

6. Throughout your real property transaction you may receive more than one disclosure form, depending upon the number of agents assisting in the transaction. The law requires each agent with whom you have more than a casual relationship to present you with this disclosure form. You should read its contents each time it is presented to you, considering the relationship between you and the real estate agent in your specific transaction.

7. This disclosure form includes the provisions of Sections 2079.13 to 2079.24, inclusive, of the Civil Code set forth on the reverse hereof. Read it carefully.

Buyer's Broker	Date	Buyer's Signature	Date
Associate License Signature	Date	Buyer's Signature	Date
Seller's Broker	Date	Seller's Signature	Date
Associate License Signature	Date	Seller's Signature	Date

------------------- *PAGE ONE OF TWO — FORM 305* -------------------

§2079.13. As used in sections 2079.14 to 2079.24, inclusive, the following terms have the following meanings:

(a) "Agent" means a person acting under provisions of Title 9 (commencing with Section 2295) in a real property transaction, and includes a person who is licensed as a real estate broker under Chapter 3 (commencing with Section 10130) of Part 1 of Division 4 of the Business and Professions Code, and under whose license a listing is executed or an offer to purchase is obtained.

(b) "Associate licensee" means a person who is licensed as a real estate broker or salesperson under Chapter 3 (commencing with Section 10130) of Part 1 of Division 4 of the Business and Professions Code and who is either licensed under a broker or has entered into a written contract with a broker to act as the broker's agent in connection with acts requiring a real estate license and to function under the broker's supervision in the capacity of an associate licensee.

The agent in the real property transaction bears responsibility for his or her associate licensees who perform as agents of the agent. When an associate licensee owes a duty to any principal, or to any buyer or seller who is not a principal, in a real property transaction, that duty is equivalent to the duty owed to that party by the broker for whom the associate licensee functions.

(c) "Buyer" means a transferee in a real property transaction, and includes a person who executes an offer to purchase real property from a seller through an agent, or who seeks the services of an agent in more than a casual, transitory, or preliminary manner, with the object of entering into a real property transaction. "Buyer" includes vendee or lessee.

(d) "Dual agent" means an agent acting, either directly or through an associate licensee, as agent for both the seller and the buyer in a real property transaction.

(e) "Listing agreement" means a contract between an owner of real property and an agent, by which the agent has been authorized to sell the real property or to find or obtain a buyer.

(f) "Listing agent" means a person who has obtained a listing of real property to act as an agent for compensation.

(g) "Listing price" is the amount expressed in dollars specified in the listing for which the seller is willing to sell the real property through the listing agent.

(h) "Offering price" is the amount expressed in dollars specified in an offer to purchase for which the buyer is willing to buy the real property.

(i) "Offer to purchase" means a written contract executed by a buyer acting through a selling agent which becomes the contract for the sale of the real property upon acceptance by the seller.

(j) "Real property" means any estate specified by subdivision (1) or (2) of Section 761 in property which constitutes or is improved with one to four dwelling units, any leasehold in this type of property exceeding one year's duration, and mobilehomes, when offered for sale or sold through an agent pursuant to the authority contained in Section 10131.6 of the Business and Professions Code.

(k) "Real property transaction" means a transaction for the sale of real property in which an agent is employed by one or more of the principals to act in that transaction, and includes a listing or an offer to purchase.

(l) "Sell," "sale," or "sold" refers to a transaction for the transfer of real property from the seller to the buyer, and includes exchanges of real property between the seller and buyer, transactions for the creation of real property sales contract within the meaning of Section 2985, and transactions for the creation of a leasehold exceeding one year's duration.

(m) "Seller" means the transferor in a real property transaction, and includes an owner who lists real property with an agent, whether or not a transfer results, or who receives an offer to purchase real property of which he or she is the owner from an agent on behalf of another. "Seller" includes both a vendor and a lessor.

(n) "Selling agent" means a listing agent who acts alone, or an agent who acts in cooperation with a listing agent, and who sells or finds and obtains a buyer for the real property, or an agent who locates property for a buyer or who finds a buyer for a property for which no listing exists and presents an offer to purchase to the seller.

(o) "Subagent" means a person to whom an agent delegates agency powers as provided in Article 5 (commencing with Section 2349) of Chapter 1. However, "subagent" does not include an associate licensee who is acting under the supervision of an agent in a real property transaction.

§2079.14. Listing agents and selling agents shall provide the seller and buyer in a real property transaction with a copy of the disclosure form specified in Section 2079.16, and, except as provided in subdivision (c), shall obtain a signed acknowledgment of receipt from that seller or buyer, except as provided in this section or Section 2079.15, as follows:

(a) The listing agent, if any, shall provide the disclosure form to the seller prior to entering into the listing agreement.

(b) The selling agent shall provide the disclosure form to the seller as soon as practicable prior to presenting the seller with an offer to purchase, unless the selling agent previously provided the seller with a copy of the disclosure form pursuant to subdivision (a).

(c) Where the selling agent does not deal on a face-to-face basis with the seller, the disclosure form prepared by the selling agent may be furnished to the seller (and acknowledgment of receipt obtained for the selling agent from the seller) by the listing agent, or the selling agent may deliver the disclosure form by certified mail addressed to the seller at his or her last known address, in which case no signed acknowledgment of receipt is required.

(d) The selling agent shall provide the disclosure form to the buyer as soon as practicable prior to execution of the buyer's offer to purchase, except that if the offer to purchase is not prepared by the selling agent, the selling agent shall present the disclosure form to the buyer not later than the next business day after the selling agent receives the offer to purchase from the buyer.

§2079.15. In any circumstance in which the seller or buyer refuses to sign an acknowledgment of receipt pursuant to Section 2079.14, the agent, or an associate licensee acting for an agent, shall set forth, sign, and date a written declaration of the facts of the refusal.

§2079.17. (a) As soon as practicable, the selling agent shall disclose to the buyer and seller whether the selling agent is acting in the real property transaction exclusively as the buyer's agent, exclusively as the seller's agent, or as a dual agent representing both the buyer and the seller and this relationship shall be confirmed in the contract to purchase and sell real property or in a separate writing executed or acknowledged by the seller, the buyer, and the selling agent prior to or coincident with execution of that contract by the buyer and the seller, respectively.

(b) As soon as practicable, the listing agent shall disclose to the seller whether the listing agent is acting in the real property transaction exclusively as the seller's agent, or as a dual agent representing both the buyer and seller and this relationship shall be confirmed in the contract to purchase and sell real property or in a separate writing executed or acknowledged by the seller and the listing agent prior to or coincident with the execution of that contract by the seller.

(c) The confirmation required by subdivisions (a) and (b) shall be in the following form:

_____ is the agent of (check one):
(Name of Listing Agent)

   ( ) the seller exclusively; or

   ( ) both the buyer and seller.

_____ is the agent of (check one):
(Name of Selling Agent if not same as above)

   ( ) the buyer exclusively;

   ( ) the seller exclusively; or

   ( ) both the buyer and seller.

(d) The disclosures and confirmation required by this section shall be in addition to the disclosure required by Section 2079.14.

§2079.18. No selling agent in a real property transaction may act as an agent for the buyer only, when the selling agent is also acting as the listing agent in the transaction.

§2079.19. The payment of compensation or the obligation to pay compensation to an agent by the seller or buyer is not necessarily determinative of a particular agency relationship between an agent and the seller or buyer. A listing agent and a selling agent may agree to share any compensation or commission paid, or any right to any compensation or commission for which an obligation arises as the result of a real estate transaction, and the terms of any such agreement shall not necessarily be determinative of a particular relationship.

§2079.20. Nothing in this article prevents an agent from selecting, as a condition of the agent's employment, a specific form of agency relationship not specifically prohibited by this article if the requirements of Section 2079.14 and Section 2079.17 are complied with.

§2079.21. A dual agent shall not disclose to the buyer that the seller is willing to sell the property at a price less than the listing price, without the express written consent of the seller. A dual agent shall not disclose to the seller that the buyer is willing to pay a price greater than the offering price, without the expressed written consent of the buyer. This section does not alter in any way the duty or responsibility of a dual agent to any principal with respect to confidential information other than price.

§2079.22. Nothing in this article precludes a listing agent from also being a selling agent, and the combination of these functions in one agent does not, of itself, make that agent a dual agent.

§2079.23. A contract between the principal and agent may be modified or altered to change the agency relationship at any time before the performance of the act which is the object of the agency with the written consent of the parties to the agency relationship.

§2079.24. Nothing in this article shall be construed to either diminish the duty of disclosure owed buyers and sellers by agents and their associate licensees, subagents, and employees or to relieve agents and their associate licensees, subagents, and employees from liability for their conduct in connection with acts governed by this article or for any breach of a fiduciary duty or a duty of disclosure.

Transactions controlled by the mandated use of the agency law disclosure form and agency confirmation provision include all four-or-less residential units and mobile-homes that are being resold.

The broker, or his agents, should make both types of agency disclosures on all types of brokerage activities, not just as mandated on one-to-four unit sales, since disclosures tend to eliminate later disputes over agency. At the very least, the broker should always confirm his agency in all purchase agreements. An agency confirmation provision establishes the agency undertaken by the broker and the relationships to be relied on in the transaction by all parties.

The agency law disclosure and the agency confirmation provision are provided by the broker at two different stages:

1. When listing property, the broker provides the sellers with an agency law disclosure form as an addendum to the listing agreement. This disclosure is not mandated to be handed to buyers when they employ a broker to locate property — but should be. [Calif. Civil Code §2079.14(a)]; and

2. When obtaining a purchase agreement offer from a buyer and an acceptance from a seller, the broker provides all parties with both:

   • the agency law disclosure as an attachment to the purchase agreement; and

   • the agency confirmation provision by filling out the provision in the purchase agreement. [CC §§2079.14; 2079.17; See **first tuesday** Form 150]

The use of the words **buyer and seller** in the agency law disclosure also refers to the tenant and landlord, respectively. Thus, the form is to be used for agency disclosures when a leasehold estate or lease of one-to-four unit residential property or mobile-homes for more than one year is created or sold.

The agency law disclosure addendum

The agency law disclosure is a two-page form. The exact wording of its entire contents is dictated by statute, and is available for all licensees to freely use. [CC §2079.16; See Form 305]

The agency law disclosure defines and explains, in general terms, many of the words and phrases commonly used in the real estate industry to express the agency relationships of:

   • brokers to the parties in the transaction;

   • broker to broker; and

   • brokers and their sales agents.

A *buyer's agent* and a *seller's agent* are mentioned but not defined. A "single agent" is not mentioned, much less defined. Clearly, the word agent in law means a licensed broker, not his agents who in fact call themselves "agents." Conversely, a broker rarely, if ever, refers to himself as an agent (which in law he is).

However, two sections on the front of the agency law disclosure form address the duties owed to parties in a real estate transaction by the undefined "seller's agent" and "buyer's agent."

The seller's listing broker is correctly noted as being an agent (broker) for the seller. Ironically, the buyer's broker is described as the *selling agent* — never described as the broker who represents the buyer.

Editors note — One wonders who, then, is the "buying agent" — an unmentioned phrase.

The addendum that contains the rules-of-agency makes no mention of and does not define brokers as "exclusive agents" for either the buyer or seller. Yet the separate agency confirmation provision in all purchase agreements provides the broker with options to denote himself as the agent of the "seller exclusively" or the "buyer exclusively."

However, the two sections on the front of the agency law disclosure entitled "Seller's agent" and "Buyer's agent" do state, in broad legal terms, generally accepted principles of law governing brokers and their conduct with the seller and buyer in a transaction.

Although the agency law disclosure does not apply these longstanding agency principles to specific brokerage activities, two categories of **broker obligations** are emphasized:

- the **primary duties** owed to a client by a broker; and

- the **general duties** owed to all parties in the transaction by each broker.

Use of the agency law disclosure

The use of the agency law disclosure is mandated to be used by real estate brokers acting as agents in **controlled property** transactions that include:

- mobilehomes; or

- one-to-four unit residential property. [CC §2079.13(j)]

However, not all transfers of interests in controlled property transactions require the use of the agency law disclosure or inclusion of the agency confirmation provision. Secured interests of lenders and borrowers under trust deeds, for example, are not yet included.

The sale, exchange or creation of interests in residential **properties controlled** by the agency disclosure law include:

- fee simple or registered ownership;

- life estates;

- existing leaseholds/leases with more than one year remaining; and

- leases created for more than one year. [CC §2079.13(l)]

The agency law disclosure must be attached to the following documents in transactions on controlled property:

- seller's listing agreement;

- landlord's authorization to lease;

- purchase agreement offer and acceptance;

- exchange agreement;

- counteroffer, directly or by reference; and

- residential lease agreement. [CC §§2079.14; 2079.17]

Transactions and negotiations concerning buyer's listings, property management (unless leases for more than one year are authorized), purchase options, financing and month-to-month rental agreements do not yet require statutory disclosure of the broker's agency to each party. The legislation is piecemeal in its approach toward creating a better informed public.

Agency rules for a seller's listing

When a seller lists controlled property, the seller's listing broker **must include** the agency law disclosure as an attachment to the seller's listing agreement. [CC §2079.14(a)]

Failure to provide the seller with the agency law disclosure prior to entering into the listing agreement results in the broker's loss of his fee if challenged by the client, even though the disclosure may be later made in a purchase agreement or escrow instructions. [**Huijers** v. **DeMarrais** (1992) 11 CA4th 676]

The agency law disclosure is also required to be used by brokers selling leasehold estates on one-to-four unit residential property leased for more than one year. [CC §§2079.13(j),(l); 2079.14]

Also, the seller's signature on the agency law disclosure is required to acknowledge receipt of a copy — even if the listing sought by the broker is not signed. [CC §2079.14]

Thus, the agency law disclosure is to be treated as a preliminary and compulsory listing event if the broker wants to enforce collection of his brokerage fee. The agency law disclosure should be signed by the seller and handed back to the broker (or his agent) before settling down to finalize the listing, which will include the disclosure as an addendum.

The broker's failure to hand the seller the agency law disclosure when the seller signs the listing agreement only affects the enforceability of the brokerage fee provision set forth in the listing. Agency obligations owed to the seller still remain enforceable against the broker.

Lack of the agency law disclosure allows the seller to cancel the listing at any time, even after the transaction sought under the listing agreement is in escrow and the brokerage fee has been further agreed to in the purchase agreement and escrow instructions.

On the other hand, the buyer's broker *perfects* the collection of his portion of the brokerage fee (if paid by the seller, not the listing broker) by including the agency law disclosure as an attachment to the purchase agreement.

Documenting a refusal to sign

If a buyer or seller should refuse to sign and return a copy of the agency law disclosure, the broker or his agent must document the refusal. [CC §2079.15]

No particular method of documenting the refusal is given by legislation or regulations. However, the facts of refusal are to be *written, dated and signed* by the broker or his agent. What is to be done with the broker's documentation of the refusal is nowhere mentioned.

The objective of disclosures seems to be to eliminate disputes which might later arise over information in the agency law disclosure form. Also, if a party claims they were never handed the agency law disclosure, the broker's written documentation of the refusal to sign would dispel such a claim.

CONFIRMATION MEMORANDUM

DATE:_____, 20_____, at _____, California

TO: _____ Company: _____ Address: _____ _____ Fax:_____	TO:_____ Company: _____ Address: _____ _____ Fax: _____

1. This memorandum confirms our conversation regarding the following contract:

   ☐ Listing/retainer agreement

   ☐ Lease/rental agreement

   ☐ Purchase agreement

   ☐ Trust deed loan number: _____

   ☐ Escrow number: _____

   ☐ Other:_____

   Dated:_____, 20_____, at _____, California

   Entered into by (name the principals): _____

   and: _____

   Regarding real estate referred to as: _____

MEMORANDUM:

2. On _____ at approximately _____ a.m./p.m.,
   you and I personally spoke:

   ☐ By phone, or ☐ In person at (place): _____

3. We agreed to the following: _____

   _____

   _____

   _____

   _____

   _____

   _____

4. Your cooperation and commitment are appreciated and will be relied upon.

5. If this memorandum does not accurately state your understanding of our conversation, please contact me immediately to correct or clarify this memorandum.

Signed and mailed this date.

Broker: _____

By (print): _____

Signature: _____

FORM 525   01-00   ©2004 first tuesday, P.O. BOX 20069 RIVERSIDE, CA 92516 (800) 794-0494

Accordingly, documentation of the facts surrounding any refusal to sign a *timely presented* agency law disclosure should be prepared on a memorandum form and retained in the broker's records. [See Form 525 accompanying this chapter, *ante*]

Further, a copy of the refusal memorandum should be mailed to all parties — including the party refusing to sign acknowledging his receipt of a copy of the agency law disclosure.

Examples of refusals to sign, though having no later effect on a brokerage fee, might occur when:

- an owner refuses to sign a seller's listing after the interview;

- a "For Sale by Owner" (FSBO) seller refuses on presentation to accept or counter, or otherwise rejects an offer to purchase; or

- a buyer refuses to sign a purchase offer that is prepared and presented by the broker for consideration.

Should a refusal to sign the agency law disclosure arise out of a failure to timely present it as an addendum to the listing or purchase agreement, the refusal is justified and cannot be overridden by later documentation.

Chapter 3

Agency confirmation provision

This article examines the use of the agency confirmation provision.

The mandated agency confirmation provision

Confirmation of agency by brokers and their agents is required to be made to all parties involved in a real estate transaction on one-to-four unit residential property, including sales, exchanges and leases of more than one year.

The agency confirmation by all brokers involved is first made as part of the purchase agreement offer, typically signed first by the buyer and then submitted to the seller.

In practice, the agency confirmation provision exists in only one format:

1. A pre-printed provision included in every purchase agreement form used in real estate transactions on one-to-four unit residential properties. [Calif. Civil Code §2079.17; See Figure 1]

The agency confirmation provision discloses the existence or nonexistence of each broker's agency with the different parties to the transaction. The **determination and declaration** of the actual agency resulting from a broker's conduct is made by each broker involved. Each broker states for which party he is acting as an agent for in the transaction.

Thus, one broker need not disclose the agency relationship of any other broker involved in the transaction. For example, the buyer's selling broker need not include the agency of the seller's listing broker when he fills out his agency confirmation provision. [CC §2079.17(a)]

Also, each time any broker prepares a purchase agreement in which he confirms his agency in the transaction, an agency law disclosure will be attached. The agency law disclosure must be presented to the buyer no later than at the time of signing a purchase offer. Further, the copy signed by the buyer must also be signed by the seller on an acceptance of an offer or a counteroffer — even though the seller has previously signed a copy as a mandated part of the sales listing agreement.

Figure 1

Excerpt from first tuesday Form 150 —
Purchase Agreement

Buyer's/ Selling Broker: _____	Seller's/ Listing Broker: _____
By: _____	By: _____
Is the agent of: ☐ Buyer exclusively, or ☐ both Seller and Buyer.	Is the agent of: ☐ Seller exclusively, or ☐ both Seller and Buyer.

The agency law disclosure is an explanation of the duties owed under the agency confirmed. [CC §2079.17(d)]

Statutory jargon

The contents of the agency confirmation provision and which agency box the broker should check requires the broker and his agents to first learn and apply the statutory definitions of:

- Agent

- Listing agent

- Selling agent

- Subagency

- Dual agency

The statutory definitions of these terms include their connotations under agency law. Under the statutes, the meanings of agency terms are oftentimes quite different from their use in brokerage jargon.

For example, by statutory definition, an *agent* is a broker who has been retained by a client, usually through the efforts of licensed sales agents employed by the broker. However, in the jargon of the real estate industry, a sales agent employed by the broker is customarily called an "agent."

By statute, the sales agent employed by a broker is defined as an *associate licensee* — an *agent of the agent,* not an agent of the client. [CC §2079.13(a),(b)]

Only the broker can be an agent of a client. Sales agents are not permitted to have clients. Sales agents are always employees

of the client's agent — the broker — even though sales agents may be classified as independent contractors for income tax purposes. [Calif. Business and Professions Code §10132]

Who is the selling agent?

The *listing agent* is also defined as being a selling agent when no other broker represents the buyer. [CC §2079.13(n)]

Remember, an agent is a broker, not a sales agent employed by a broker. Thus, the listing office/broker is also the selling broker when no other broker is involved and the listing office is "double-ending" a transaction — even though the broker confirms he is the exclusive agent of the seller with no agency duties owed to the buyer. [See Figure 2]

A selling agent by definition is now a legal schizophrenic with four distinct personalities, each of the four being a different type of agency relationship. [CC §2079.13(n)]

The definition of selling agent includes situations commonly called "selling office" or "selling broker" in the daily practice of brokerage. The definition of a selling agent does not include the listing office's associate licensee, a sales agent, who might be dealing with a buyer on behalf of the broker. However, the real estate industry presently refers to an associate of the broker who has contact with a buyer as the "selling agent."

However, only the broker can legally be the *selling agent*. The broker's sales agent is acting on his behalf.

Selling agent now includes the following four types of agency relationships:

1. The seller's listing broker, when acting as the seller's exclusive agent and no other broker is involved in the transaction acting on behalf of the buyer. [See Figures 2 and 4]

2. Other brokers who work with the seller's listing broker to locate a buyer, or who are authorized and instructed by the seller's listing broker to act as a subagent of the seller to also locate buyers. [See Figure 5]

3. Brokers locating property for buyers, including single agency and fee-splitting (cooperating) brokers. [See Figure 3] and

4. Brokers locating buyers for an owner of unlisted property, a For Sale by Owner (FSBO). [CC §2079.13(n)]

Note in the four definitions above the two objectives of each broker's solicitation:

- *locating property* for a buyer; or

- *locating buyers* for a property.

The solicitation criteria establish the *client* for whom the broker works.

For example, a broker who is retained by a buyer is said to have listed the buyer or been retained by his buyer. By agency definition, this buyer's broker now is a *selling agent*. In practice this broker is also called a "single agent" or "buyer's broker."

As a selling agent, the buyer's broker confirms his agency in the purchase agreement as "the agent of the buyer exclusively" — even though no oral fee arrangements, much less a written exclusive right-to-buy listing, may exist with the buyer. [See Figure 1]

Of course, the buyer's broker might find his agency confirmation complicated by having a listing with the seller of the property on which his buyer makes an offer. Thus, the broker becomes a *dual agent*. Dual agency is confirmed by checking the box for agent of "both the buyer and seller." [See Figures 1 and 4]

When two brokers are involved in a sales transaction, the seller's broker (the listing agent) and his client (the seller) will be asked to accept and sign a purchase agreement with the agency confirmation prepared by the buyer's broker. However, the buyer's broker might state a type of agency the seller's listing broker or the seller does not want to create with the "selling broker." Thus, a counteroffer will be prepared to clarify the agency relationships which exist.

Use of the agency confirmation provision

Both the agency confirmation provision in purchase agreements and the separate agency law disclosure are required as part of a purchase agreement on all *offers and acceptances* negotiated by brokers to buy, sell, exchange, or lease for more than one year property that includes one-to-four residential units or mobilehomes. [CC §2079.17(d)]

Accordingly, transactions involving four-or-less residential units and mobilehomes that require both the agency confirmation provision and the agency law disclosure prior to obtaining signatures include:

- **an offer** to buy, exchange or lease for more than one year [CC §§2079.14; 2079.17(a)]; and

- **an acceptance** of an offer to buy, exchange or lease, whether presented by:

  1. The selling broker as agent to the seller [CC §§2079.14(b); 2079.17(a),(b)]; or

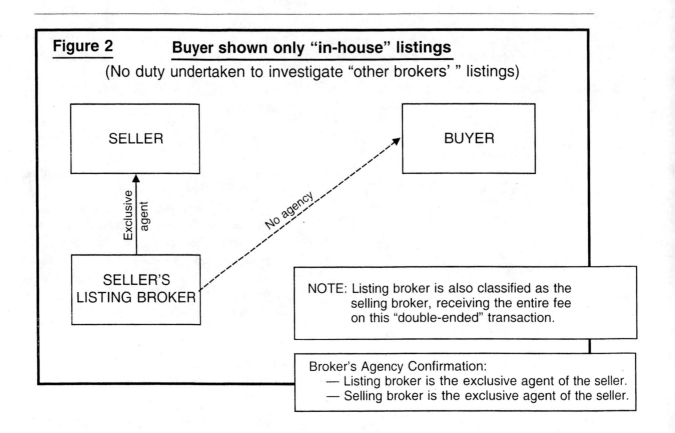

Figure 2   **Buyer shown only "in-house" listings**
(No duty undertaken to investigate "other brokers' " listings)

SELLER

BUYER

Exclusive agent

No agency

SELLER'S LISTING BROKER

NOTE: Listing broker is also classified as the selling broker, receiving the entire fee on this "double-ended" transaction.

Broker's Agency Confirmation:
— Listing broker is the exclusive agent of the seller.
— Selling broker is the exclusive agent of the seller.

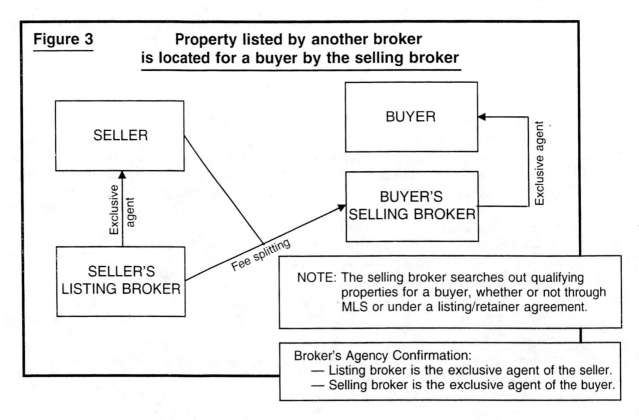

Figure 3   **Property listed by another broker**
is located for a buyer by the selling broker

SELLER

BUYER

Exclusive agent

BUYER'S SELLING BROKER

Exclusive agent

Fee splitting

SELLER'S LISTING BROKER

NOTE: The selling broker searches out qualifying properties for a buyer, whether or not through MLS or under a listing/retainer agreement.

Broker's Agency Confirmation:
— Listing broker is the exclusive agent of the seller.
— Selling broker is the exclusive agent of the buyer.

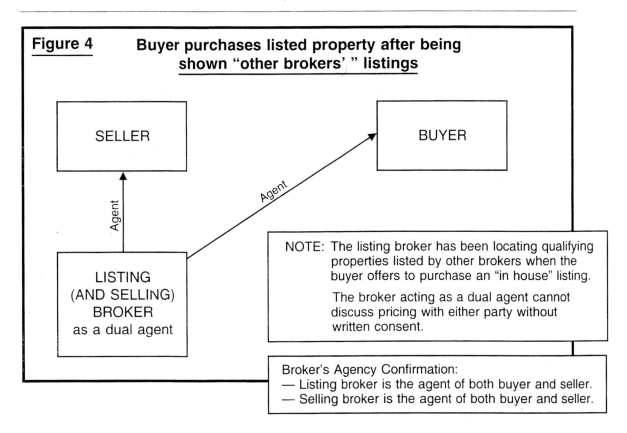

Figure 4   Buyer purchases listed property after being shown "other brokers' " listings

SELLER

BUYER

Agent

Agent

LISTING (AND SELLING) BROKER as a dual agent

NOTE: The listing broker has been locating qualifying properties listed by other brokers when the buyer offers to purchase an "in house" listing.

The broker acting as a dual agent cannot discuss pricing with either party without written consent.

Broker's Agency Confirmation:
— Listing broker is the agent of both buyer and seller.
— Selling broker is the agent of both buyer and seller.

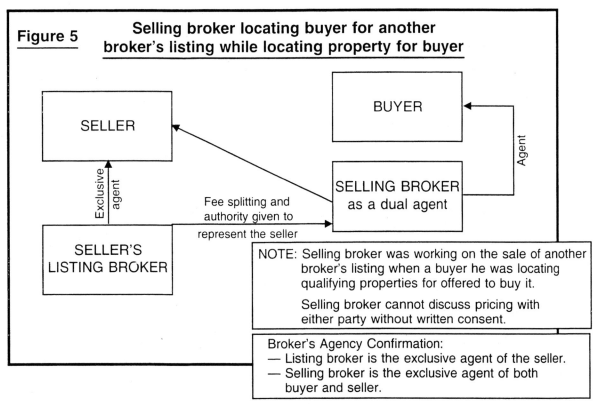

Figure 5   Selling broker locating buyer for another broker's listing while locating property for buyer

SELLER

BUYER

Agent

Exclusive agent

SELLING BROKER as a dual agent

Fee splitting and authority given to represent the seller

SELLER'S LISTING BROKER

NOTE: Selling broker was working on the sale of another broker's listing when a buyer he was locating qualifying properties for offered to buy it.

Selling broker cannot discuss pricing with either party without written consent.

Broker's Agency Confirmation:
— Listing broker is the exclusive agent of the seller.
— Selling broker is the exclusive agent of both buyer and seller.

2. The listing broker on behalf of the selling broker who is not a subagent of the seller. If the seller's signature acknowledging receipt of the agency law disclosure attached to the buyer's offer is not obtained by the listing broker, the buyer's selling broker may send a copy to the seller by certified mail to eliminate the need for a signed acknowledgment by the seller. [CC §§2079.14(c); 2079.17(a),(b)]

In practice, when a selling broker (or his agent) prepares and presents a purchase agreement offer to the buyer for his signature, the broker will:

1. Hand the buyer the agency law disclosure.

2. Present the buyer with the purchase agreement containing an agency confirmation provision, along with a review of the purchase price, terms of payment and property conditions.

3. Obtain the buyer's signature on the agency law disclosure and the purchase agreement.

If the seller counters on a counteroffer form that incorporates all the provisions of the buyer's offer, the seller has signed a writing which includes (by reference) the confirmation of the broker's agencies. All the seller needs to sign is the counteroffer and the agency law disclosure.

Likewise, should the seller reject the buyer's offer by a counteroffer prepared on a new purchase agreement form, the seller still needs to sign the agency law disclosure.

Double-ending codified

When only the seller's listing broker or his agents are involved in a transaction, they typically do not undertake the agency task of working with the buyer to locate suitable property, other than a property from their "in-house" listings. [See Figure 2]

When no attempt is made to represent the buyer in locating outside listings or unlisted property, the seller's broker is strangely defined as being both the listing agent and the selling agent — but only for the purposes of making agency disclosures, not to become the buyer's agent.

Ironically, when a broker is said to have "double-ended" a deal, only one broker is involved and only one brokerage fee is paid. What is meant by this phrase is that no "cooperating" selling broker was involved with whom the fee will be split (co-oped).

In practice, the "one-broker" transaction that does not include a dual agency merely requires the listing broker to include an agency law disclosure and confirm his agency as the "exclusive agent of the seller" — an agency confirmation which is part of all purchase agreement provisions. [See Figure 1]

After a broker confirms his agency, it may need to be changed. Should a broker or any party determine the confirmed agency needs to be corrected, a change can be made prior to close of escrow.

To make the change, an agency confirmation statement should be prepared and signed by all parties and brokers involved. A statement should be added, noting that the agency confirmation statement represents a modification of an earlier agency confirmation entered into in the transaction. [CC §2079.23; See Form 306 accompanying this chapter]

AGENCY CONFIRMATION STATEMENT

DATE:_____, 20_____, at _____, California

Items left blank or unchecked are not applicable.

FACTS:

1. This confirmation is an addendum to the following:

    ☐ Purchase agreement

    ☐ Exchange agreement

    ☐ Counteroffer

    ☐ Lease agreement

    ☐ Escrow

    NOTICE:

    This broker agency confirmation complies with the agency disclosure required with offers for the purchase, sale, exchange or over-one-year lease of one-to-four residential units and mobilehomes. [Civil Code §2079.17]

    Dated:_____, at _____ , California,

    entered into by _____

    and _____,

    regarding real estate referred to as: _____

    _____

    _____

CONFIRMATION:

2. _____

   (NAME OF SELLER'S/LISTING AGENT)

    is the agent of (check one): ☐ the Seller exclusively; or

    ☐ both the Buyer and Seller.

3. _____

   (NAME OF BUYER'S/SELLING AGENT if not the listing agent)

    is the agent of (check one): ☐ the Buyer exclusively; or

    ☐ both the Buyer and Seller.

4. The attached Agency Law Addendum is a part of this confirmation. [**first tuesday** Form 305]

5. Should an over-one-year lease or leasehold interest be involved, the Tenant and Landlord are referred to as the Buyer and Seller, respectively.

My agency is as stated above.	**My agency is as stated above.**
Buyer's/ Selling Broker: _____	Seller's/ Listing Broker: _____
By: _____	By: _____
Address: _____	Address: _____
_____	_____
Phone: _____	Phone: _____
I agree to the above stated agency or agencies.	**I agree to the above stated agency or agencies.**
Date:_____, 20_____	Date:_____, 20_____
Buyer: _____	Seller: _____
Buyer: _____	Seller: _____

FORM 306   10-00   ©2004 **first tuesday**, P.O. BOX 20069 RIVERSIDE, CA 92516 (800) 794-0494

Preparing the agency confirmation statement

Identification: **Enter** the date and city where this agreement is prepared. This is the date used to reference this document.

Facts:

1. **Check** the appropriate box to identify the agreement to which this addendum is attached. **Enter** the date and city where the agreement was prepared. **Enter** the names of the parties to the agreement. **Enter** the property description.

Confirmation:

2. *Seller's/listing agent agency confirmation*: **Enter** the name of the broker with whom the property is listed, called the *listing agent*. **Check** the appropriate box to confirm the agency of the listing agent to the parties in the transaction.

3. *Buyer's/selling agency agency confirmation*: **Enter** the name of the broker representing the buyer, called the *selling agent*, unless the broker also is the listing broker. **Check** the appropriate box to confirm the agency of the selling agent to the parties in the transaction.

4. *Agency law disclosure*: Attached is the mandatory agency law disclosure to be handed to and signed by both the buyer and seller.

5. *Use for leaseholds:* States the tenant and landlord on a lease exceeding one year are referenced as the buyer and seller, respectively.

Signatures:

Selling Broker: **Enter** the name of the buyer's broker. **Obtain** the signature of the buyer's broker or his selling agent. **Enter** the broker's address and phone number.

Listing Broker: **Enter** the name of the seller's broker. **Obtain** the signature of the seller's broker or his listing agent. **Enter** the broker's address and phone number.

Buyer(s): **Enter** the date the buyer signs the agreement. **Obtain** the signature(s) of the buyer(s).

Seller(s): **Enter** the date the seller signs the agreement. **Obtain** the signature(s) of the seller(s).

Chapter 4

Subagency and dual agency

This chapter distinguishes subagency and dual agency, and examines the conduct required of a dual agent.

Creation of subagency or dual agency

The payment of the brokerage fee due a buyer's broker by the seller or seller's broker does not determine the agency relationship of the buyer's broker to the parties. Conversely, words in an acceptance provision separate from the buyer's offer in a purchase agreement stating the seller agrees to employ the buyer's broker as his broker establishes the buyer's broker as an agent of the seller.

Thus, the seller's payment of the brokerage fee due the buyer's broker, either directly to the buyer's broker or by assignment of an agreed-to portion of the fee received by the seller's/listing broker (and without words of employment), does not create either a subagency or a dual agency. [Calif. Civil Code §2079.19; See Figures 3 and 5 accompanying Chapter 3]

Typically, brokers working for buyers to locate suitable property do not consider themselves agents of the seller when they show their clients properties listed with other brokers — nor do they behave like subagents of the seller or dual agents for both seller and buyer. [See Figure 3 accompanying Chapter 3]

Fee splitting by the listing broker, or payment by the seller of the buyer's brokerage fee, whether or not a member of a Multiple Listing Service (MLS), does not make the buyer's broker a dual agent.

Subagency and MLS membership

A broker's membership in an MLS creates neither a dual agency nor a subagency relationship with the principals (sellers) of other broker-members of the MLS. Agency, whatever the type, is created by the conduct of each broker (and his agents) with the parties to a transaction. [CC §2307]

The word "subagent," as used in real estate jargon, has become badly distorted by MLS members statewide to the point that reference to a subagency often infers brokerage conduct which is the antithesis of the word's legal meaning.

The legal aspects of subagency duties differ greatly from MLS subagency concepts which arise out of cooperation in fee-splitting arrangements.

For example, when an MLS selling broker believes he is a "subagent" in a transaction on property listed by another broker, the critical brokerage facts include:

- the selling broker is an MLS member;

- the buyer has been assisted by the selling broker to locate all suitable qualifying property;

- the buyer has signed a purchase offer prepared by the selling broker to buy property listed with another broker; and

- the brokerage fee due the selling broker will be paid by the seller based on a fee-splitting offer made in MLS publications by the listing broker to share his fee with any member-broker who has a buyer that submits an offer at the listed price and terms.

This set of selling agent facts is also referred to in the MLS "subagency" environment as "cooperation," "cooperating office," "cooperating agent," "selling office" or by the code "SO." The selling broker choosing to be paid on a fee-splitting basis with the seller's broker does so by accepting (or rejecting) the offer for the percentage stated in the SO (selling office) fee codes in MLS printouts — if the buyer agrees to pay the price on the terms sought in the MLS publication.

When a buyer works with his broker's "selling agent" and makes an offer on an "in-house" listing taken by another agent employed by the **same broker**, the agent who obtained the listing is referred to as the "listing agent." In practice, when the words selling agent or listing agent are used to identify a licensee, it always is a reference to a sales agent employed by a broker. However, it is the broker who is the *legal agent* of the client, the sales agent being the *agent of the agent*.

Occasionally, MLS brokers locating property on behalf of a buyer wrongfully believe they are subagents of the seller (or dual agents), and believe so for the wrong reason — fee-splitting cooperation. More important than their mistaken belief, a buyer's broker does not perform any of the acts on behalf of the seller which are legally required of actual subagents (or dual agents). [See Figure 4 accompanying Chapter 3]

In fact, a selling broker always refers to his buyer as "my client." However, the "in-house" selling agent of a listing broker also loosely refers to any potential buyer as "my client" even when agency duties owed to a client have not yet been undertaken, or may never be undertaken. In which case, the buyer is not a client at all. [See Figure 2 accompanying Chapter 3]

The buyer's exclusive selling agent

A buyer's broker typically reviews an extensive number of qualifying properties and supporting data to assist his buyer in making the correct choice about which property to acquire, if any. Also, buyer's brokers freely use any legitimate business or negotiating advantage they or the buyer has against the seller.

Conversely, this buyer's agent does not pass information on to the seller (who they usually have not met), or to the seller's broker concerning the buyer's intention in the negotiations, such as price, terms, financial or tax motivation, ulterior reasons for contingencies, etc.

Specifically, any *personal information* known about the buyer that might possibly provoke the seller to counteroffer is kept confidential by the buyer's broker — the essence of being the agent of *the buyer exclusively*.

As against a seller, buyer's brokers actively negotiate for the best business advantage available to the buyer on pricing, down payment, loans, carryback interest rates, due dates and conditions regarding title and improvements.

Buyer's brokers correctly attempt to shift to the seller as much of the buyer's acquisition costs, new loan costs, and property improvement or maintenance costs as possible, as well as the liberty to confirm the buyer's expectations with contingencies for further approval based on inspection, etc., or cancel the transaction.

Simply put, buyer's brokers are not acting as legal subagents of the seller or as dual agents. They are "gumshoes," marshalling information and their expertise in the best interests of their client, the buyer. [See Figure 3 accompanying Chapter 3]

If the buyer's broker acts with any less personal involvement, the buyer will instinctively want to seek out another broker who manifests greater fidelity toward the buyer.

Subagent vs. cooperating broker

A seller's listing agreement usually authorizes the listing broker *to cooperate* with other brokers *and divide* with them any brokerage fees due under the listing. [See **first tuesday** Form 102 §5.2]

Listing agreements do not usually include additional wording that authorizes the seller's listing broker to *delegate to other brokers the authority to also act as the seller's agent to locate buyers and obtain offers to purchase*, an activity called *subagency.*

However, if the listing does authorize the creation of a subagency to help further market the property, the seller's broker may employ a subagent to also act on behalf of and in direct contact with the seller. The listing agent does so by specifically delegating to another broker the power to act as an additional agent of the seller to locate buyers under the listing, called a *seller's subagent.* [CC §2349]

It is critical to understand the buyer's circumstances when a subagency exists before you can appreciate the multiplicity of agency roles which exist in California. [See Figures 3 and 5 accompanying Chapter 3]

Subagency facts include:

- two separate brokers, one being a seller's/listing broker and the other a "selling broker";

- a seller who is exclusively represented by the listing broker; and

- a buyer who is not exclusively represented (or possibly not represented at all) by the selling broker. [See Figure 5 accompanying Chapter 3]

For example, a selling (buyer's) broker is working for a buyer, sorting through qualifying properties to locate one suitable for the buyer to acquire. However, the broker shows the buyer a property listed by another broker he has been working with as a *subagent* of the seller to locate buyers for the property under the existing listing.

On presentation of the property to his buyer, the broker becomes a dual agent — he has been assisting the listing broker to locate buyers. Having become a dual agent, the selling broker cannot now exchange pricing information between the buyer, the seller or the seller's/listing broker if the property is a one-to-four unit residential property. [CC §2079.21]

However, the listing broker remains the exclusive agent of the seller and is free to actively pursue the collection of data and information regarding the price and the terms the buyer might be willing to agree to — and deliver the data and information directly to the seller. [CC §2079.13(n)]

This unbalanced circumstance is improperly imposed on some transactions by brokers (and their agents) due to their misconception that a legal subagency arises due to fee splitting (cooperating) and MLS membership.

A buyer's broker may tend to erroneously believe he is automatically the seller's subagent when the fee is to be paid by the seller. However, fee splitting or any other method of compensation does not create a subagency nor any other agency. [CC §2079.19]

In listing agreements, the words "cooperate with other brokers" do not authorize the listing broker to employ a subagent who is answerable directly to the seller. Also, a subagent/selling broker established by the listing broker is not an agent of the listing broker — allowing the listing broker to use information collected by the subagent to the detriment of the buyer.

Also, most listings authorize publication and dissemination of property information in an MLS and other marketing mediums.

However, doubt still persists at the MLS level: Does publication of the property profile, its price, and the broker's offer to fee split with buyer's/selling brokers automatically create a subagency (or dual agency) for the selling broker with the seller?

It does not!

Selling broker as exclusive agent for seller

Rarely will the selling (buyer's) broker need to check the agency confirmation provision stating he is the agent for "the seller exclusively," unless the broker:

- is the listing and only broker in the transaction; and

- has not presented the buyer with properties other than those he has listed.

For example, brokers working with buyers to locate qualifying properties are hard pressed to acknowledge they work exclusively for the seller — so they do not. For a selling broker to declare he is the "seller's agent exclusively," the broker is telling the buyer that the buyer is not his client and that the primary agency duties owed to a client to obtain the best business advantage and to give advice on the legal, tax, financial and risk of loss aspects of the transaction as they relate to the buyer are not duties he owes to the buyer.

In practice, buyers develop confidence in the agents they work with. The confidence is often built up during an agonizing process of locating and selecting suitable property.

Natural allegiances arise between buyers and brokers (or their agents) when the buyer is shown properties other than just the broker's "in-house" listings. The buyer's only face-to-face contact from property to property is with this broker. These circumstances develop the buyer's confidence to rely on the advice and recommendations of the broker — the heart of an agency.

The most likely agency confirmation provision checked by selling brokers who do not have a listing on the subject property will be as agent of "the buyer exclusively."

It is less likely the selling broker will need to check the agency confirmation box representing he is a dual agent for "both the buyer and seller."

Dual agency vs. exclusive agency

Dual agency is denoted in the agency confirmation provision in purchase agreements as the agent of "both the buyer and seller."

The use of the term "exclusive agent" to designate a broker's agency duties for a buyer or a seller is noted in the agency confirmation as the only alternative to dual agency.

Exclusive agency has been chosen by the legislature to be the uniform term for what has developed in practice as "single agency," "buyer's broker" or YKYIKM ("you-keep-yours, I-keep-mine). Generally, these terms have been used in the past to indicate each broker will be paid by the client he represents.

No legal precedent or statute caused these "paid-by-the-client" features of agencies to come about. These features, in practice, will certainly persist for those who want to clarify the broker's relationship with his client, as against the other party who usually is the seller. However, these "buyer's brokers" are now classified by the agency statutes as "exclusive agency" situations — no matter who pays his fee. They are legally referred to as "selling agents" even though their task is to be the "buying agent" locating property for the buyer, not selling property to the buyer (as do listing agents).

Exclusive agency for the buyer can be practiced by brokers whether they are paid by their client, by the opposing broker or the opposing broker's client. Selling brokers and their agents will confirm their agency as "exclusive" for the buyer they represent in the transaction (unless they are the listing broker). The mechanics of collecting the fee is a separate matter from agency.

Interestingly, and at the same time confusing, a broker operating under an "exclusive listing" with either the seller or the buyer does not automatically become the exclusive agent of the client in future transactions.

When negotiating a purchase agreement, an agency confirmation given as "the exclusive agent" to the client is a result of the broker's lack of an agency relationship with other parties to the transaction. Only in the future, after a listing has been taken and when a transaction has been negotiated with a buyer, will the extent of a broker's agency relationship to each party be able to be established — and then confirmed in the purchase agreement.

Brokerage restrictions as dual agent

In the past, a broker acting as a dual agent was required to "tell all" to both parties he represented, acting as a sort of "open book" or two-way conduit for information on the transaction. The buyer and seller legally and literally had no secrets withheld from each other by their dual agent regarding material facts affecting the transaction and known to the broker.

Their intentions regarding the pricing, terms of payment, financing, use of the property, ability to close escrow, personal finances or other factors which provided strength or weakness in the negotiating process were passed on to all parties by the dual agent broker.

The dual agent was a "conduit" through which all facts affecting negotiations or closing would pass to the other side.

However, under agency disclosure law regarding transactions on one-to-four unit residential property, the legislature did much more than establish rules requiring disclosure of the various types of broker-client agency relationships. The law controlling the "conduct" of dual agents in these transactions was changed.

Now, when a dual agency results and both sides of a one-to-four unit residential transaction are represented by the same broker, the broker (and his agents) may not pass any information relating to the price or terms of payment from one party to the other. What price the buyer may be willing to pay or the seller may be willing to accept must remain the undisclosed knowledge of the dual agent. [CC §2079.21]

Thus, the dual agent is now a "secret agent" — he must keep secret the minimum pricing sought by the seller or maximum pricing obtainable from the buyer.

Timely confirmation of agency

Consider a seller who lists a one-to-four unit residential property for sale with a real estate broker.

Without the seller's written permission, the broker tells a prospective buyer, for whom he is presently acting as an agent to locate property, that the seller will accept a price lower than the listed price.

The buyer makes an oral offer to purchase the property at the lower price. The broker convinces the seller to accept the buyer's offer, orally assuring the seller he is the seller's exclusive agent and is acting in the seller's best interest. A written purchase agreement is not prepared.

Escrow instructions are prepared and the seller signs the instructions without reading them. An addendum to the instructions discloses the dual agency of the broker. After closing, the seller takes time to read the instructions and discovers the dual agency disclosure for the first time.

The seller makes a demand on the broker for the difference between the listing price and the lesser price he received for the property. The seller claims the broker is responsible for the loss since the broker had an affirmative duty to timely bring his dual agency to the attention of the seller.

The broker claims he is not liable for the seller's loss since the seller signed the escrow instructions that disclosed the broker's dual agency.

Is the broker liable for the seller's losses?

Yes! The seller is entitled to recover the difference between the listing price and the sales price since confirmation of the dual agency in the escrow instructions was untimely. The time for confirmation (in writing) is when the offer is submitted, even though it was an oral offer to purchase. [**Brown** v. **FSR Brokerage, Inc.** (1998) 62 CA4th 766]

Also, a broker acting as a dual agent in a transaction involving one-to-four unit residential property must have written authority from the seller before relaying **pricing information** to the buyer. [CC §2079.21]

For instance, if the seller of one-to-four unit property will accept less than the listed price, this information cannot be released to the buyer by a dual agent unless written consent is received from the seller.

Conversely, if the broker acting as a dual agent knows the buyer will pay more than his initial offer, the broker (and his agents) cannot now release this information to their seller-client without written consent from the buyer.

The decision not to release pricing information must be made and maintained from the moment the dual agency arises — a moment which always occurs before the purchase agreement and its agency confirmation provision is prepared.

The authority to advise the seller of the buyer's willingness to pay more, or the seller to accept less, is best documented in a modification of listing form signed by the client whose confidential pricing information is being released. The authority would be given to the broker and the document would be retained in his file. [See **first tuesday** Form 120]

While at first glance pricing disclosures may seem unnecessary, negotiations with a seller or a buyer do frequently require some inducement to generate a counteroffer when the prior offer or counteroffer is unacceptable. Then the written authority to release pricing information may be helpful.

Dual agency as an authorized practice

Simply put, a dual agent is a broker who is acting as the agent for opposing parties in a transaction — typically the buyer and the seller. [CC §2079.13(d)]

The past and future problem with dual agents is not that dual agency is improper — dual agency has been and is proper brokerage practice. It is that a dual agency must be disclosed in the agency confirmation provision in the purchase agreement. [CC §2079.17]

Further, a broker on any type of real estate transaction who fails to promptly disclose his dual agency is subject to the loss of his brokerage fee, liability for his clients' money losses and disciplinary action by the Department of Real Estate (DRE). [Calif. Business and Professions Code §10176(d)]

For example, a buyer's broker locates property his buyer is interested in purchasing. Without disclosing his existing agency relationship (oral or by conduct) with the buyer, the broker enters into a written listing agreement with the seller. The buyer makes an offer which the seller accepts. In the offer, the seller agrees to pay the broker a fee.

Before closing, the seller discovers the broker's prior relationship with the buyer and cancels payment of the brokerage fee. The broker demands his fee for locating the buyer.

However, the broker cannot recover a brokerage fee. The broker intentionally failed to disclose his dual agency to the seller at the time he entered into the listing with the seller. [**L. Byron Culver & Associates** v. **Jaoudi Industrial & Trading Corp.** (1991) 1 CA4th 300]

Once a broker becomes a dual agent, he (and his agents) typically do not know how to perform as a dual agent, usually due to a lack of training.

A rule of sorts for disclosure of relevant facts about the transaction which come to the dual agent's attention, either before or after acceptance of an offer, is to advise both parties of the facts by memorandum and keep a copy of the memo in the broker's file.

To illustrate the point, consider a broker who is employed under a listing to sell real estate. The broker locates a buyer who enters into a purchase agreement with the seller. Later, to facilitate the closing, the broker agrees to and loans the buyer the down payment needed to purchase the property.

The seller learns of this loan and refuses to pay the brokerage fee. The broker makes a demand for the fee, claiming he performed all of the services required prior to making the loan. The seller claims the broker is not entitled to a fee since the broker's failure to disclose the downpayment loan violated the fiduciary duty the broker owed to the seller.

Is the broker still entitled to his brokerage fee in light of the breach?

Yes! The broker is entitled to a brokerage fee, but sanctioned by a small reduction. The broker's failure to disclose the downpayment loan was an omission of a material fact and a breach of the fiduciary duty owed to the seller. However, it was neither an intentional breach nor due to bad faith on the broker's part and did not harm the seller. [**In re Mehdipour** (9th Cir. BAP 1996) 202 BR 474]

Confusion over handling **backup offers** received during escrow is a common occurrence in dual agency situations. The confusion arises over whether the backup offer should be presented to:

- the seller, who is in escrow having already sold the property; or

- the buyer, who will receive title and is the only one who can now sell and deliver the property; or

- both?

A dual agent must disclose any significant activity regarding the property to both the buyer and seller, including backup offers that occur prior to the close of escrow.

Thus, any offers from others to purchase which are received by a dual agent prior to the closing of a sale must be presented to both seller and buyer — unless the broker has instructions from the seller or buyer stating they are not interested in receiving offers from third parties.

Dual agency and diminished benefits

Generally, the clients of a dual agent lose some assistance they would have received from an exclusive agent. The conflicts which exist in a broker's dual representation rule out aggressive negotiations to obtain the best business advantage for either party. This holds true even if different agents employed by the same broker each work with different parties to the same transaction. [**Timmsen** v. **Forest E. Olson, Inc.** (1970) 6 CA3d 860]

While a broker owes his client the duty to pursue the best business advantage legally and ethically obtainable through negotiations and agreements, the dual agent is foreclosed from achieving this advantage for either client. The dual agent cannot take sides with one or the other principal in negotiations.

A natural inability exists to negotiate the highest and best price for the seller and at the same instant negotiate the lowest and best price for the buyer. Further, the broker and his agents, while acting as dual agents, are precluded in sales transactions on one-to-four unit residential property from using any pricing discussion for or against the parties without their prior written approval.

The agent for a buyer or seller in a transaction is the broker, not his sales agent or associated brokers. For this reason, in-house transactions make it particularly difficult to handle dual agency negotiations. Typically, one of the broker's agents acquires the listing while another agent separately works with a buyer to locate qualifying properties listed with other brokers. Thus, their broker becomes a dual agent when the buyer decides to buy an in-house listing after having reviewed other brokers' listings or unlisted property with an agent in the office. [See Figure 4 accompanying Chapter 3]

What will occur and will not be easy for brokers who are dual agents to supervise, is the discussions with clients the broker's agents will have on the touchy topic of what price the seller will take and just what price the buyer will pay.

Agents of the dual agent broker instinctively talk to one another, passing on the intent and desires of their respective "in-house" clients. This discussion between "in-house" agents is permitted no differently than had the agents or the clients relayed their pricing intention directly to the broker.

But what is impermissible in one-to-four unit residential sales transactions, without prior written consent authorizing the release of a party's pricing instructions, is for the broker's agents to pass on any further pricing information to the opposing party — their broker is a "dual agent" in the sale of a one-to-four unit residential property.

Another improper tendency in transactions involving only one broker and two of his agents who are handling the listing and sales aspects of the transaction is to automatically designate the broker as a dual agent.

In fact, the buyer probably is a party to whom no primary agency duties are owed. The buyer probably responded to the broker's "For Sale" sign or ads on listed property, made an offer on an "in-house" listing without being shown properties listed with other brokers and the offer accepted.

When the buyer's inquiry and the broker's review of properties with the buyer is limited to properties listed by the broker, this action on in-house listings does not, by itself, create an agency relationship with the buyer. [**Price v. Eisan** (1961) 194 CA2d 363]

There remains, as always, the broker's *general duty* to all parties, including the non-client buyer, to make full and meaningful disclosures about the condition of the property's physical aspects, hazards, location, title and operations (income or expenses) that might affect the buyer's decision to purchase the property.

Chapter 5

A broker's use of supervisors

This chapter explains the broker's continuing responsibilities when delegating his supervisory duties to an office manager or transaction coordinator.

Supervision delegated, not agency

A sales agent employed by a broker is the agent of the broker, not the client. In turn, the broker is the agent of the client.

As an agent representing the broker, a real estate sales agent is authorized to prepare listings, sales documents, disclosure sheets, etc., on behalf of the broker.

The Department of Real Estate's (DRE) **supervisory scheme** requires the broker to reasonably supervise a sales agent's activities. Reasonable supervision includes establishing policies, rules, procedures and statements to review and manage:

- transactions requiring a real estate license;

- documents having a material effect upon the rights or obligations of a party to the transaction;

- the filing, storage and maintenance of documents;

- the handling of trust funds;

- advertisement of services that require a license;

- sales agent's knowledge of anti-discrimination laws; and

- the reports of the activities of the sales agents. [Department of Real Estate Regulation §2725]

The broker may employ others to carry out his supervisory responsibility to review documents and maintain files, including:

- another licensed real estate broker; or

- a real estate sales agent employed by the broker. [DRE Reg. §2725]

The review of documents and file maintenance should not just be a mechanical function, but should be a meaningful review to locate errors such as in mathematical computations, contract and escrow provisions and completeness and timeliness of disclosures.

The broker, office manager or transaction coordinator reviewing documents must see to it the sales agent cures any unacceptable documentation at the earliest possible moment.

Should time pass without corrective activity, and the parties to the transaction change their positions — i.e., close escrow — the broker is exposed to greater liability for any money damages caused by the sales agent's error.

A **written agreement** concerning the employment of other licensees to carry out the broker's responsibility for managing the activities of sales agent's on a sale, lease or loan should be entered into between the broker and the manager or transaction coordinator. [See Form 510 accompanying this chapter]

OFFICE MANAGER EMPLOYMENT AGREEMENT

DATE:_____, 20_____, at _____, California

Broker hereby employs licensee as the Office
Manager of Broker's real estate office located at:

_____

_____

Department of Real Estate Regulation §2725(b) allows Broker to delegate his responsibility and authority over licensees in his employ to a licensed broker or to a licensed salesman who has two years full-time experience during the past five years.

1. OFFICE MANAGER AGREES TO:

1.1 Maintain a real estate license in the State of California and act as Office Manager for Broker.

1.2 Provide managerial/supervisory service under the direction of the Broker or the Designated Officer in Broker's employ.

1.3 Diligently perform duties assigned and immediately deposit and account to Broker for all cash or checks received by Office Manager or employees assigned to him.

1.4 Develop a working relationship with each licensee employed at this office.

1.5 Assist in the implementation of Broker's policy manual and any other directions given by Broker.

1.6 Review all correspondence and documents made or received by Broker or his agents.

1.7 Participate in any educational programs or meetings specified by Broker.

1.8 Assure a full inspection and disclosure of the conditions of any property to be sold, bought or encumbered by Broker's clients.

1.9 Obligate Broker to no agreement without Broker's prior consent.

1.10 Expose Broker to no liability to any third party without Broker's prior consent.

1.11 Join and pay fees for Office Manager's membership in any professional organization in which Broker is a member.

1.12 Divulge to no one the business or names of clientele, lists or descriptions of forms, trade secrets or business practices of Broker during or after the term of this agreement.

1.13 ☐ Also be employed by Broker as an independent contractor. Concurrent herewith, Office Manager and Broker have entered into and signed a separate independent contractor's form. [**first tuesday** Form 506]

    a. Any conflicts in the terms of these agreements shall be controlled by this agreement.

2. BROKER AGREES TO:

2.1 Create the necessary resolutions to adopt this agreement.

2.2 Maintain a license as a real estate broker in the State of California.

2.3 Maintain an office with proper facilities to operate a real estate brokerage business.

2.4 Maintain membership in the following professional organization(s):

    ☐ Multiple Listing Service
    ☐ Local branch of the California Association of Realtors and National Association of Realtors
    ☐ _____

2.5 Maintain listings.

2.6 Provide advertising approved by Broker.

2.7 Provide worker's compensation insurance for Office Manager.

2.8 Maintain the following insurance coverage for Office Manager:
    ☐ Errors and Omissions ☐ Health
    ☐ Dental   ☐ Life ☐ Other: _____

2.9 Indemnify Office Manager for the expense of any legal action arising out of the proper performance of Office Manager's duties.

— — — — — — — — — — — — — *PAGE ONE OF TWO — FORM 510* — — — — — — — — — — — — — —

2.10 Pay Office Manager as specified in the Office Manager's fee schedule, section 3 of this agreement.

2.11 Withhold from the Office Manager's compensation all appropriate state and federal income taxes, state disability insurance, and social security taxes.

2.12 Other: _____

3. OFFICE MANAGER'S FEE SCHEDULE:

3.1 The Office Manager is to be compensated under this agreement solely for his administrative efforts.

3.2 Broker shall pay Office Manager monthly, on the tenth business day following the end of each calendar month of employment, _____% of Broker's share of gross fees, after deducting any portion earned by Broker's agents, other Brokers and any Franchisor, received in the brokerage business during the preceding calendar month.

3.3 The fee schedule may be changed by Broker on 30 days prior written notice to Office Manager.

3.4 On termination, Office Manager will be paid on a pro rata basis for any period of employment he has not been compensated.

4. TERMINATION:

4.1 This agreement shall continue until termination by mutual written agreement, or 30 days after either party serves written Notice of Termination, or either party, for cause, serves written Notice of Termination.

4.2 For one year after termination, Office Manager will not interfere with Broker's continuing relationship with his clients and employees, nor induce or attempt to induce any sales staff to discontinue representing Broker for the purpose of representing another broker.

4.3 For one year after termination and within 25 miles of the office, Office Manager is not to become employed with any real estate brokerage business, nor employ or become employed with any real estate licensee who was employed by Broker during the six months prior to termination.

5. GENERAL PROVISIONS:

5.1 Broker reserves the exclusive right to determine whether any dispute involving the Broker and third parties and arising from Office Manager's performance of assigned duties, shall be prosecuted, defended or settled.

5.2 ARBITRATION: Any dispute between Office Manager and Broker or any other licensee employed by Broker which cannot be resolved by the Broker or State Labor Commission shall be arbitrated under the rules of the American Arbitration Association.

5.3 ☐ **See addendum for additional terms.**

OFFICE MANAGER:	**BROKER:**
I agree to render services on terms stated above.	**We agree to employ Office Manger on terms stated above.**
Date:_____, 20_____	Date:_____, 20_____
Name: _____	Broker: _____
Social Security Number: _____	Officer's Name: _____
Signature: _____	Title: _____
Address: _____	Signature: _____
_____	Address: _____
Phone: _____	Phone: _____
Fax: _____	Fax: _____
E-mail: _____	E-mail: _____

FORM 510   10-01   ©2004 **first tuesday**, P.O. BOX 20069 RIVERSIDE, CA 92516 (800) 794-0494

Figure 1

*Excerpt from **first tuesday** Form 510 — Office Manager Employment Agreement*

1.6 Review all correspondence and documents made or received by Broker or his agents.

While the office manager or transaction coordinator is assigned administrative duties, their primary responsibility is to review all correspondence and documents made or received by the agents on behalf of the broker. [See Figure 1]

No liability avoidance

Even though the broker uses an office manager or transaction coordinator, the broker has the overall supervisorial responsibility to review the acts of the office manager, transaction coordinator and each sales agent. [DRE Reg. 2725]

Real estate sales agents and broker associates employed as agents of a broker are under the direct supervision of their broker and remain so even if an office manager or transaction coordinator actually performs the supervision.

The actions of a sales agent and broker associate are considered the acts of the employing broker. [Calif. Civil Code §2079.13(b)]

Sales agent employment agreement

A real estate broker must have a written employment agreement with each of his sales agents.

A sales agent is defined as someone employed by a real estate broker. The licensee may be a sales agent or a broker. [Calif. Business and Professions Code §10132]

The agreement must provide for the supervision of the agent's activities, fulfillment by the sales agent of the duties owed by the broker to clients and the public, and the sales agent's compensation.

The broker is mandated by law, subject to suspension or loss of his license, to perform constant and substantial supervision over his sales agents. [B & P C §10177(h)]

Supervision of nonlicensed individuals

A broker employed as a property manager may employ nonlicensed individuals to perform administrative-type property management duties.

Under the supervision of a licensed real estate broker who has been retained to **manage an apartment building or complex**, a nonlicensed employee of the broker may:

- show rentals;

- provide and accept preprinted rental applications;

- accept deposits, fees and rents;

- give information about the rental schedule and provisions contained in the rental/lease agreement, under written instruction from the broker; and

- receive signed lease/rent agreements from prospective tenants. [B & P C §10131.01]

The broker may employ others to carry out his responsibility to supervise the activities of his nonlicensed employees, including:

- another licensed real estate broker; or

- a real estate sales agent employed by the broker, if the sales agent has at least two years full-time experience as a sales agent licensee during the preceding five-year period. [DRE Reg. §2724]

The broker's delegation to the office manager or transaction coordinator of the responsibility to supervise his nonlicensed employees must be included in a written agreement. [See Figure 1]

Office manager liability

The office manager may also be an agent representing the broker. Like a sales agent or nonlicensed employee, the office manager who meets with the client or other parties is representing the broker in a transaction.

While acting as an office manager or transaction coordinator, the licensee owes a duty to supervise only to the employing broker. The broker, in turn, is responsible to the client for any breach in agency duty caused by the office manager's or transaction coordinator's failure to supervise and correct an agent's errors or omissions. However, the office manager or transaction coordinator may have to indemnify the broker for failure to supervise as agreed. [**Walters** v. **Marler** (1978) 83 CA3d 1]

While most supervisory responsibility can be assigned to an office manager or transaction coordinator, the agency duty the broker owes to a client in a transaction cannot be delegated to others, and the broker's agency obligations cannot be avoided. [**Barry** v. **Raskov** (1991) 232 CA3d 447]

Thus, the broker cannot use an office manager or transaction coordinator as a means of evading responsibility for the acts of his agents by delegating the performance of his supervisory duties or by delegating to the office manager or transaction coordinator his agency obligation owed to clients and the public.

SECTION C

FAIR HOUSING

Chapter 1

The Federal Fair Housing Act

This chapter examines the federal prohibitions against discriminatory activity in the sale, lease or advertisement of residential dwellings.

Introduction to fair housing

The Fair Housing material is designed to provide real estate licensees with:

- knowledge of federal and state fair housing laws relating to the sale and rental of real estate;

- knowledge of selected federal and state civil rights and anti-discrimination laws relating to real property transactions and business establishments;

- the ability to avoid practices that could be construed as discriminatory in commercial and residential transactions and facilities; and

- the need for real estate brokers to be committed to the affirmative compliance with the fair housing laws.

Emphasized in this course is the federal and state housing laws which relate to the sale and rental of property, such as prohibitions against redlining, discriminatory advertisement, refusing to show properties and blockbusting.

On completing the reading, a real estate licensee will be familiar with the requirements and restrictions against discriminatory housing practices.

Anti-discrimination legislation for residential property

The Federal Fair Housing Act (FFHA) prohibits discrimination in:

- the sale, rental or advertisement of **dwellings**;

- offering and performing **brokerage services**;

- making **loans** to buy, build, repair or improve a dwelling;

- the **purchase** of real estate loans; or

- **appraising** real estate. [42 United States Code §§3601 et seq.]

A **dwelling** includes any building or structure that is occupied or designed to be occupied as a residence by one or more families, and any vacant land offered for sale or lease for the construction of a residential building or structure. [42 USC §3602(b)]

Discriminatory actions of a broker or sales agent are any actions which are based on a person's:

- race or color;

- national origin;

- religion;

- sex;

- familial status; or

- handicap. [42 USC §3602]

Familial status refers to one or more individuals who are under the age of 18 and live with:

- a parent or person having legal custody; or

- a person having written permission of the parent or legal custodian as the designee of the parent or custodian. [42 USC §3602(k)]

Handicap refers to persons who have:

- a physical or mental impairment which substantially limits the person's life activities; or

- a record of or are regarded as having physical or mental impairment. [42 USC §3602(h)]

The term handicap does not include the current illegal use of a controlled substance. However, individuals who are considered "recovering or recovered addicts" are protected as handicapped. [**United States** v. **Southern Management Corporation** (4th Cir. 1992) 955 F2d 914]

Also, individuals with the Human Immunodeficiency Virus (HIV) are protected as handicapped. [24 Code of Federal Regulations §100.201; See Chapter 12]

Refusal to sell or rent

A broker is prohibited from discriminating in the negotiations and the handling of an offer in the sale or rental of a dwelling. [42 USC §3604(a)]

Thus, a broker may not:

- **refuse to sell or rent** a dwelling or to negotiate for the sale or rental of a dwelling for discriminatory reasons;

- **impose different charges** in the sale or rental on a dwelling for discriminatory reasons;

- discriminate in the use of qualification **criteria or applications** in the sale or rental of a dwelling; or

- **evict a tenant** or the tenant's guests for discriminatory reasons. [24 CFR 100.60(b)]

Different *criteria* or *applications* when qualifying an individual include a broker's use of different income standards, credit analyses, or sale or rental approval procedures in the sale or rental of a dwelling. [24 CFR 100.60(b)(4)]

For example, a broker is hired by a residential apartment owner to perform property management activities. One of the broker's duties as a property manager is to locate tenants to fill vacancies.

A minority tenant contacts the broker about the availability of an apartment.

The broker informs the minority tenant of the monthly rent.

When the prospective minority tenant asks the broker for an application, the broker informs him a nonrefundable fee is charged to process the application. The minority tenant fills out the application.

Later, a non-minority tenant inquires about the rental of the same apartment unit. The monthly rental rate the broker quotes is much lower than the rental rate quoted to the minority tenant.

Further, the non-minority tenant is not charged a fee for filling out the application. Also, the non-minority tenant is not as creditworthy as the minority tenant. The apartment is then rented to the non-minority tenant.

The broker's actions are a violation of the FFHA. The higher rates, charges and qualification criteria imposed on the minority tenant are construed to be **racially motivated**. Based on the tenant's race, the broker misrepresented the rental terms of the apartment by using different procedures and qualification standards in accepting and processing the tenant's application. [**United States** v. **Balistrieri** (7th Cir. 1992) 981 F2d 916]

Different terms, conditions, privileges, services and facilities

A broker may not discriminate in the **terms, conditions or privileges** of the sale or rental of a dwelling, or in providing **services and facilities** to dwellings. [42 USC §3604(b)]

For example, a prospective buyer who is a member of a minority group responds to an advertisement concerning the sale of a residence in a new housing development.

The broker shows the buyer the residence. The minority buyer informs the broker he is interested in purchasing the property.

The broker informs the buyer he cannot sell the home to the minority buyer since it would become more difficult to sell the remaining homes in the development.

The broker further states the developer who owns the development is more than willing to build an identical house at the same price in another part of town, an activity called *steering*.

Here, the broker has discriminated against the prospective minority buyer. The broker has refused to sell the house in a particular location to the buyer due to the buyer's race. [**United States** v. **Pelzer Realty Company, Inc.** (5th Cir. 1973) 484 F2d 438]

Prohibited activities in the terms, conditions, privileges, services and facilities offered on the sale or rental of dwelling units include a broker's activities with *intent to discriminate* by:

- using **different provisions** in lease or purchase agreements, such as in rental charges, security deposits, terms of the lease, down payment and closing requirements;

- **delaying or failing** to perform maintenance or repairs;

- limiting an individual's use of privileges, services or facilities; or

- refusing or failing to provide services or facilities due to a person's refusal to provide sexual favors. [24 CFR §100.65(b)]

When a dwelling is available, a broker may not discriminate by representing that the dwelling is not available for inspection, sale or rent in order to redirect individuals to a particular neighborhood, called *steering*.

Steering involves the restriction of a person seeking to buy or rent a dwelling in a community, neighborhood or development in a manner that perpetuates segregated housing patterns. [24 CFR §100.70; 42 USC §3604(d)]

Discrimination in advertisement

A broker may not print, publish or make any notice, advertisement or statement which indicates a *preference, limitation or discrimination* in the sale or rental of a dwelling. [42 USC §3604(c); See Chapter 4]

The prohibition against discriminatory advertisements applies to all **oral and written** statements. Written notices and statements include any applications, flyers, brochures, deeds, signs, banners, posters and billboards used in the sale of a dwelling.

Blockbusting

A broker, whether acting as an agent or as a principal, unlawfully discriminates if he induces or attempts to induce an owner to sell or rent a dwelling by representing that the entry of certain classes of people into the neighborhood will have an adverse economic effect on property values or rental rates, called *blockbusting*. [42 USC §3604(e)]

Further, an actual profit is not necessary for discrimination to have occurred, provided profit was a motive for the blockbusting activity. [24 CFR §100.85]

Examples of blockbusting activities include:

- actions which convey the neighborhood is undergoing, or is about to undergo, a change in the race, color, religion, sex, handicap, familial status or national origin of its residents in order to encourage an owner to offer a dwelling for sale or rent; or

- encouraging an owner to sell or rent a dwelling by making the assertion the entry of persons of a particular race, color, religion, sex, familial status, handicap or national origin will result in undesirable consequences for the neighborhood or community and increase criminal activity, or cause a decline in the schools and other facilities. [24 CFR 100.85(c)]

Real estate related transactions

A real estate broker may not discriminate in other real estate related transactions, including:

- **making or purchasing loans** used to purchase, construct, improve, repair or maintain a dwelling, or a loan secured by residential real estate; or

- **selling, brokering or appraising** residential real estate. [42 USC §3605]

Further, discrimination in membership in an Multiple Listing Service (MLS), brokerage organization or other service related to selling or renting dwellings is prohibited by the FFHA. [42 USC §3606]

Aiding in discriminatory activities

An individual may not coerce, intimidate, threaten or interfere with any person in the exercise or enjoyment of a dwelling. [42 USC §3617]

For example, a mobilehome park that is subject to local rent control ordinances operates as an "adults-only" park. However, the park owner never qualified the park as a senior citizens housing development exempt from the FFHA.

Later, a local ordinance is passed freeing the park from local rent restrictions when renting to new residents. The park owner then decides to fill vacancies by opening the park to families with children.

Tenants who currently rent mobilehomes in the park and are subject to rent control restrictions file a complaint with the city. The tenants seek a rent reduction, claiming the families with children will cause a reduction in services. The city awards the existing tenants the reduction in rent.

The park owner claims the city violated the FFHA since it interfered with his decision to rent to families with children.

The city claims it did not violate the FFHA since the park actually met the requirements of a senior citizen housing project and thus was exempt from the FFHA.

Did the city interfere with the park owner's rental of the mobilehomes to families with children?

Yes! The tenants without families are not entitled to a rent reduction since the city established two tiers of rental amounts based on **familial status**, a violation of the FFHA. The city interfered with the park owner's rental of the mobilehomes to families with children by requiring the park owner to reduce the rent to tenants without children. Further, only an owner can claim the park is exempt from the FFHA under the senior housing exemption. [**United States** v. **City of Hayward** (9th Cir. 1994) 36 F3d 832]

Exemptions from the FFHA

Discrimination law covering the sale or rental of a residential dwelling does not apply to a single-family house sold or rented by an owner who:

- does not own more than three single-family homes;

- does not live in the house at the time it is sold and is not the most recent resident if the house is the owner's only sale of a residential dwelling in the past 24 months;

- does not retain the services of a real estate broker or salesman or any other person **in the business** of selling or renting dwellings; and

- does not publish, post or mail any discriminatory advertisements. [42 USC §3603(b)(1)]

Thus, the FFHA does apply to all **notices, statements and advertisements** in the sale or rental of a dwelling. [42 USC §3603]

An owner, broker or sales agent is **in the business** of selling or renting dwellings if the individual:

- has participated within the past 12 months as a **principal** in three or more transactions involving the sale of real estate;

- has participated within the past 12 months as an **agent**, by providing sales or rental services in two or more transactions involving the sale or rental of any dwelling or interest in a dwelling, excluding the broker's or agent's personal residence; or

- is the owner of a dwelling intended to be occupied by five or more families. [42 USC §3603(c)]

Thus, if a broker is the agent for any of the parties to a sale or rental transaction, the FFHA applies to the sale.

However, attorneys, escrow agents, title companies and professionals other than brokers who are necessary to complete the transaction are not considered real estate professionals which would bring the transaction under the FFHA. [42 USC §3603(b)(1)(B)]

Also exempt from discrimination rules in the sale or rental of a dwelling is a **one-to-four unit** residential rental property in which the owner lives in one of the units. [42 USC §3603(b)(2)]

Religious organizations may limit the sale, rental or occupancy of dwellings, provided the dwelling is owned for noncommercial reasons, to individuals of the same religion, unless the religion is restricted to persons of a particular race, color or national origin. [42 USC §3607(a)]

Also, **a private club** which is not open to the public and that operates dwellings for noncommercial purposes may limit rental or occupancy of the dwellings to its members.

Finally, housing for older citizens is not considered discrimination based on familial status. However, the housing project must first be qualified as housing for older persons. [42 USC §3607(b); See Chapter 4]

Failing to comply with the FFHA

An aggrieved person is any person who claims to have been injured by a discriminatory housing practice or believes he will be injured by a discriminatory housing practice. [42 USC §3602(i)]

Any aggrieved person may file a complaint alleging a discriminatory housing practice with the Secretary of Housing and Urban Development (HUD). The complaint must be filed within one year of the alleged discriminatory housing practice. [42 USC §3610(a)]

After informal negotiations, the Secretary will attempt to have the parties enter into an agreement resolving the dispute. [42 USC §3610(b)]

However, a judicial action may be required to resolve the issue of discrimination if the Secretary concludes it is necessary. The dispute will then be resolved by an administrative law judge. However, any party to the complaint may elect to have the claims decided in a civil action. [42 USC §3612(a)]

If neither party elects to have the dispute resolved in a civil action, then the administrative law judge will hear the complaint. If the administrative law judge finds a discriminatory housing practice has or is about to take place, the administrative law judge may award actual damages caused by the discriminatory housing practice, an injunction or other equitable relief against the discriminatory housing practice, plus civil penalties in the amount of:

- no more than $10,000 if the person has not been previously adjudged to have participated in discriminatory housing practices;

- no more than $25,000 if the person has been adjudged as participating in discriminatory housing practices within five years of the current complaint being filed; or

- no more than $50,000 if the person has been adjudged to have participated in two or more discriminatory housing practices within seven years of the current complaint being filed.

However, if the person who is adjudged to have committed prior acts of housing discrimination is a natural person, then the penalties may be assessed without regard to the time limits of prior adjudication. [42 USC §3612(g)(3)]

Further, if a real estate broker is found to have committed discriminatory housing practices, the Secretary will notify the Department of Real Estate (DRE) and recommend disciplinary action. [42 USC §3612(g)(5)]

If in a civil action the court determines discriminatory housing practices have taken place, the court may award actual and punitive damages and may issue an injunction, temporary restraining order or other order preventing the person from engaging in any discriminatory housing practice. [42 USC §3613(c)(1)]

Further, if the Attorney General commences a civil action against a person for discriminatory housing practices, the court may award:

- relief preventing further discriminatory housing practices, such as an injunction or restraining order;

- money damages; and

- civil penalties of no more than $50,000 for the first violation and no more than $100,000 for any subsequent violation. [42 USC §3614(d)]

Chapter 2

The Civil Rights Acts of 1866 and 1870

This chapter presents the federal scheme that assures all races the equal right to sell, purchase or lease property without discrimination.

Property rights cannot be based on race

All citizens of the United States have the right to purchase, lease, sell, hold and convey real estate and personal property, regardless of race. [42 United States Code §1982]

Further, all persons within the United States, legally or illegally, have the same rights to make and enforce contracts, sue, be sued, enjoy the full benefits of the law and be subject to the same punishments, penalties, taxes and licenses, regardless of race. [42 USC §1981]

The protection against race discrimination given under *The Civil Rights Acts of 1886 and 1870* applies to discrimination generally, and is much broader than the protection given under *The Federal Fair Housing Act. The Civil Rights Acts of 1886 and 1870* apply to race discrimination on **all types of real estate**, not just residential real estate.

In addition, the right to lease, sell, hold and convey real estate is further protected by giving all persons the right to make and enforce contracts regardless of race. Contracts in real estate transactions include purchase agreements, leases, trust deeds, grant deeds and quitclaim deeds.

Thus, racially motivated actions in any real estate related transaction are prohibited.

For example, a city housing authority is to construct low-income public housing.

The city housing authority, through inverse condemnation, acquires an area which is considered integrated, and levels the existing structures to build high-rise public housing.

The community in the surrounding area in which the public housing is to be built opposes the construction of high-rise public housing. Instead, the city housing authority decides to construct single-family homes as public housing.

The city condemns more property to build the single-family residences. As a result, the area surrounding the proposed development becomes all white.

The single-family housing project is approved by local community representatives. Later, as construction begins, the community representatives decide to oppose the project. The community representatives block access to the construction site and the equipment so the development cannot be completed.

The city's mayor then actively opposes the construction of the public housing. The mayor implies the public housing will be black housing and does not belong in the white neighborhood.

The city then decides to terminate the housing project.

Does the city violate an individual's right to real estate because of racc?

Yes! The city is racially motivated in opposition to the project. The city was originally passive in support of the project, then it actively sought to prevent the development after the citizens of the area initiated biased demonstrations.

As a result, the city is prohibited from interfering with the completion of the public housing project. The city, with discriminatory intent, delayed and frustrated the public housing project that would have allowed the area to become integrated. [**Resident Advisory Board** v. **Rizzo** (1977) 564 F2d 126]

Chapter 3

Americans with Disabilities Act

This chapter reviews the accommodations businesses and nonresidential landlords must make for disabled persons.

Providing access to nonresidential real estate

An employer may not discriminate against a *qualified person with a disability* who seeks employment based on the person's disability under the *Americans with Disabilities Act (ADA)*. [42 United States Code §12112]

A broker is an **employer** if he has 15 or more employees each working day during a period of 20 or more calendar weeks occurring in either the current or the preceding calendar year. [42 USC §12111(5)(A)]

For the purposes of the ADA, **employees** include all representatives of the broker, such as broker associates, sales agents, managers, administrative personnel and call center employees.

A **disability** includes:

- a physical or mental impairment that limits one or more of a person's major life activities;

- a record of such an impairment; or

- being regarded as having such an impairment. [42 USC §12102(2)]

A disabled person is considered a *qualified person with a disability* if the person can perform a job with or without reasonable accommodation by the employer.

Further, a person with a disability cannot be discriminated against in the offering of public services, or in places of public accommodation or commercial (nonresidential) facilities. [42 USC §§12132; 12182(a)]

Public accommodations and commercial facilities

Places of *public accommodation* and *commercial facilities* must be designed, constructed and altered in compliance with the ADA. [28 Code of Federal Regulations §36.101]

Real estate is considered a place of public accommodation if it is owned, leased or operated by a private entity and the operation affects commerce. Thus, a place of **public accommodation** includes:

- an inn, hotel, etc., unless it contains five or fewer rooms for rent and is occupied by a resident manager;

- establishments serving food or drink (i.e., restaurants or bars);

- places of exhibition, entertainment or public gathering (i.e., theaters, stadiums, convention facilities);

- sales or other service establishments (i.e., grocery stores, clothing stores, dry cleaners, brokerage offices, insurance offices, doctors offices);

- public transportation depots;

- a place of public display or collection (i.e., museums, libraries);

- places of recreation (i.e., zoos, parks);

- places of education;

- social service center establishments (i.e., day care centers, senior citizen centers); and

- places of exercise or recreation (i.e., gymnasiums, health spas, golf courses).

A **commercial facility** is:

- intended for nonresidential use; and

- its operation affects **commerce**. [42 USC §12181]

Commerce is travel, trade, traffic, transportation or communication:

- among several states;

- between a foreign country or any territory and a state; or

- within a state but through another state or foreign country. [42 USC §12181]

Any person who owns (landlords) or operates (businessmen) a place of public accommodation or a commercial facility may not *discriminate* on the basis of a disability. [42 USC §12182(a)]

Discrimination includes:

- use of eligibility requirements that screen out individuals with disabilities;

- failure to make reasonable modifications in policy, practices or procedures necessary to provide accommodations;

- failure to take the steps necessary to ensure a person with a disability is not excluded, denied services, segregated or treated differently in the accommodations offered;

- failure to remove architectural and communication barriers which are structural in nature and where such removal is readily achievable; and

- with respect to a facility that is altered, failing to make alterations which provide accessibility to persons with disabilities. [42 USC §§12182(b)(2)(A); 12183]

Both a landlord who owns a place of public accommodation and a tenant who operates a place of public accommodation are subject to the ADA. In a lease provision, the landlord and tenant may agree who is responsible for complying with the ADA. [28 CFR §36.201]

Removal of architectural and communication barriers

A place of public accommodation is required to provide necessary aids, such as telecommunication devices (TDD), closed-caption decoders, etc., to ensure effective communication with individuals with disabilities. This rule is subject to a reasonableness standard. Thus, compliance is not required if it would place an undue burden or significant difficulty or expense on the public accommodation. [28 CFR §36.303]

For example, a public accommodation is not required to use telecommunication devices for the deaf (TDDs) for receiving or making telephone calls incidental to operations. [28 CFR §36.303(d)]

However, places of public accommodation providing lodging in which televisions are placed in five or more guest rooms must provide closed-caption decoders for the hearing impaired on request. [28 CFR §36.303(e)]

A place of public accommodation must remove architectural barriers which limit access for disabled persons.

Examples of the removal of **architectural barriers** include:

- installing ramps;

- making curb cuts for wheelchair access;

- rearranging furniture; and

- widening doors. [28 CFR §36.304(b)]

Penalties for violation

Any person who has been discriminated against based on their disability may seek a court order to stop the discriminatory activity or practice. Further, the individual may file a claim with the Attorney General who may seek monetary and civil penalties.

Civil penalties may be assessed against an individual who discriminates based on a person's disability in the amount of:

- $50,000 for the first violation; and

- $100,000 for each subsequent violation. [42 USC §12188(b)(2)(C)]

Also, portions of residential real estate used as a place of public accommodation, and any portion used for both residential purposes and as a place of public accommodation, are subject to the ADA. The portion of the real estate used exclusively for residential purposes is controlled by *The Federal Fair Housing Act*. [28 CFR §36.207; See Chapter 1]

Chapter 4

California's civil rights laws

This chapter discusses the obligation of residential and nonresidential business establishments to avoid discriminatory conduct toward members of protected groups.

The Unruh Civil Rights Act

An owner of a unit in a condominium project (CID) brings a child into the unit. The project does not qualify as senior citizen housing, but its covenants, conditions and restrictions (CC&Rs) limit residency to persons over the age of 18. The project's homeowner's association (HOA) is a nonprofit organization and has the authority to enforce the CC&Rs.

The HOA notifies the owner of the CC&R violation and demands the child be removed, which the owner refuses to do. The HOA then seeks to have the owner ejected for failure to remove the child.

The owner claims he and the child may remain in the project since the **age restriction** in the CC&Rs is unenforceable as a violation of California's anti-discrimination law.

The HOA claims California anti-discrimination law does not apply to the association since it is a nonprofit business establishment.

Is enforcement of the age restrictions in the CC&Rs by a nonprofit HOA a violation of California's anti-discrimination law?

Yes! The HOA is barred by California statutes from discriminating against a person because of age since it is a business establishment. The HOA is considered a business establishment since it performs all the customary business functions **typical of a landlord** in a landlord/tenant relationship.

Further, the HOA is not excluded from being considered a business establishment due to its status as a nonprofit organization. [**O'Connor** v. **Village Green Owners Association** (1983) 33 C3d 790]

Anti-discrimination

California's *Unruh Civil Rights Act* specifically prohibits discrimination by a **business establishment** because of a person's sex, race, color, religion, ancestry, national origin, disability or medical condition. However, age restrictions can be enforced in a project that qualifies as a **senior citizen housing** development. [Calif. Civil Code §§51; 51.2; 51.3]

California's anti-discrimination law applies to anyone in the business of providing housing or any nonresidential real estate facility. Brokers, housing developers, apartment owners, condominium owners and single-family residential owners are considered to be in the business of providing housing.

Further, a business establishment may not boycott, blacklist, refuse to buy from or sell to or enter into contracts because of the race, creed, religion, color, national origin, sex, disability or medical condition of a person, the person's partners, members, stockholders, directors, officers, managers, agents, employees, business associates or customers. Thus, no person or organization may be blacklisted or boycotted for these discriminatory reasons. [CC §51.5]

Reasonable vs. arbitrary discrimination

The state's civil rights and fair housing laws prohibit a broker from practicing any out-lawed discrimination when locating tenants for a residential or nonresidential property.

However, discriminatory standards which are **reasonably related** to the operation of the income property are valid. This includes distinguishing criteria to ensure a prospective tenant is financially able to pay the rent and will not damage or put the property to an improper use.

Further, standards which are applied equally to all individuals and do not discriminate against **protected groups** are more likely to be considered reasonable.

Generally when providing services, the broker must avoid distinguishing among tenants for reasons such as age, sex, religion, foreign language, education, color or marital and familial status.

Housing for older persons

Provisions in a written instrument which prohibit or restrict the conveyance, encumbrance, lease, use or occupancy of residential or nonresidential real estate due to a persons sex, race, color, religion, ancestry, national origin, age or disability are void, and thus of no effect. [CC §53]

However, a provision in a written instrument which refers to qualified senior citizen housing is enforceable as allowable age discrimination.

Senior citizen housing is housing:

- intended for and **solely occupied** by persons 62 years of age or older; or

- intended for and **occupied by at least one person** of 55 years of age or older. [42 United States Code §3607(b)]

Landlords and owners of retirement communities or senior citizen apartment complexes can exclude children to meet the particular needs of older persons.

To qualify as senior citizen housing under the *Unruh Civil Rights Act*, a project must be developed, substantially renovated or rehabilitated for senior citizens and consist of at least 35 dwelling units. [CC §51.3]

However, California legislation does recognize the special design requirements for senior housing may be difficult for developments constructed before 1982 to meet. Thus, any housing development **constructed before February 8, 1982** may be considered a senior citizen housing development if the development meets all the requirements of a senior citizen housing development except the requirement the housing be specially designed to meet the physical and social needs of senior citizens. [CC §§51.2(a); 51.4]

Qualifying for senior citizen housing under the FFHA

A "62-or-older" senior housing exemption from anti-discrimination law is contained in the *Federal Fair Housing Act (FFHA)*. Property qualifies as senior housing if it is occupied only by persons who are 62 years of age or older. The 62-or-older restriction **excludes all persons** under the age of 62, even if one spouse is 62 or older and the other is not. [24 Code of Federal Regulations §100.303(b)]

Older housing projects qualify under the exemption even though persons under the age of 62 reside on the premises provided the underage persons were living on the premises as of September 13, 1988. However, all vacancies in the project after September 13, 1988, must be occupied exclusively by persons 62 or older. [24 CFR §100.303(a)(1),(2)]

Further, the housing project can qualify even though project **employees and their families** living on the premises are under 62 years of age. To qualify as employees they must perform substantial duties directly related to the management or maintenance of the housing. [24 CFR §100.303(a)(3)]

If a project owner elects not to qualify or cannot qualify for the 62-or-older exemption, the project can still qualify under the broader 55-or-older exemption.

The 80% rule for 55-or-older

At least 80% of the rented units must be occupied by at least one person 55 or older.

For newly constructed projects, the 80% occupancy requirement does not apply until the real estate is 25% occupied. [24 CFR §100.305(d)]

The 55-or-older rule does not apply to residents who occupied the project on September 13, 1988, as long as at least 80% of new vacancies are occupied by an individual who is 55 years old or older. [24 CFR §100.305(e)(1)]

Spouses may live with their 55-or-older spouse in apartment and condominium pro-jects under California's *Unruh Civil Rights Act* since the FFHA leaves age restrictions regarding those under 55 to the states.

For example, under California law, a person may occupy a residential unit, other than a mobilehome, with a person 55-or- older if the younger person:

- resides with the 55-or-older person prior to the senior's death, hospitalization or dissolution of marriage with; **and**

- is 45 years old, a spouse, or a person offering primary economic or physical support for the 55-or-older occupant; or

- is a child or grandchild of the 55-or-older occupant with a disability, illness or injury. [CC §51.3(b)(2),(b)(3)]

Mobilehomes are subject to California's Mobilehome Residency Law which states age discrimination in mobilehome parks must comply with the FFHA. Thus, the mobilehome park cannot discriminate against a younger co-tenant since federal law does not allow any discrimination, provided one occupant is at least 55 years of age. [CC §798.76]

Penalties for discrimination

A broker who discriminates is liable for damages of no less than $1,000 and no more than three times the amount of the tenant's actual money losses, plus any attorney fees. [CC §52(a)]

Chapter 5

Fair housing for disabled persons

This chapter discusses California's prohibition against barriers that interfere with equal access to housing accommodations by disabled persons.

Full and equal access to residential rental units

A blind tenant seeks to rent a unit in a landlord's apartment building. The tenant has a guide dog.

The landlord refuses to rent an apartment to the blind tenant, claiming the guide dog violates the building's pet restriction.

The blind tenant claims the landlord is discriminating against him based on his disability, and the landlord may not deny him housing becàuse of the guide dog.

Is the tenant correct?

Yes! A landlord may not refuse to rent residential property to a **blind tenant** due to the tenant's guide dog. This also applies to deaf and other disabled persons who use **specially trained dogs** to assist them. [Calif. Civil Code §54.1(b)(6)]

Fair housing for disabled persons

California law prohibits discrimination against disabled persons when renting or leasing residential real estate. Under California law, **a disabled person** is defined as anyone who:

- has a physical or mental impairment that significantly limits major life activities;

- has a record of a disability; or

- is regarded as being disabled. [CC §54(b)]

People with disabilities are entitled to full and equal access to housing accommodations offered for rent. [CC §54.1(b)(1)]

The only exception is when no more than one room is rented in a single-family residence. [CC §54.1(b)(2)]

The case of the blind tenant with the guide dog is one example of ways in which landlords might seek to evade the anti-discrimination laws. A landlord may attempt to justify his refusal to rent to a blind tenant with a guide dog based on his pet restriction. Yet, the refusal to rent to a disabled tenant is still unlawful discrimination.

Also, the landlord may not charge a **security deposit** for a disabled tenant's guide dog. [CC §54.2]

However, a landlord with a pet restriction policy is not required to rent an apartment to a disabled tenant with a dog if the dog is not specially trained to assist the tenant. [CC §54.1(b)(5)]

Also, the landlord may impose reasonable regulations on the presence of the dog. Further, the tenant is liable for any property damage caused by the dog.

Now consider a disabled tenant who is dependent on his spouse for financial support. The disabled tenant and his spouse seek to rent an apartment. The tenant and his spouse will both sign the lease agreement.

The spouse's income meets the landlord's minimum income requirement which reasonably relates to the ability to pay the rent amount.

The landlord refuses to rent the couple an apartment, claiming the disabled tenant does not meet minimum income requirements.

However, the landlord may not deny housing to the disabled tenant based on the tenant's financial dependency on his spouse. The **combined income** of the tenant and his spouse meets minimum income requirements.

The landlord's refusal to rent an apartment to the disabled tenant based on the tenant's dependence on his spouse's income is unlawful discrimination. [CC §54.1(b)(7)]

Accommodations for disabled persons

A landlord is not required to modify existing residential rental property to meet the special needs of disabled tenants. [CC §54.1(b)(4)]

Although he is not required to modify the property for a disabled tenant, the landlord must allow the tenant to make **reasonable modifications**. The landlord may require the tenant to **restore the property** to its original condition when the tenancy is terminated. [Calif. Government Code §12927]

Also, anti-discrimination law requires **new residential properties** of four-or-more-units per building (i.e., large apartment buildings) to be built to allow access to disabled persons. Required adaptations include wheelchair ramps and kitchens and bathrooms designed to allow access to disabled tenants.

Failure to provide disabled access to a four-or-more-unit residential property is considered unlawful discrimination. [Gov C §12955.1]

Remedies

The primary remedy for discrimination based on a physical disability is to seek a court ordered injunction against the discriminatory activity. The injunction may be sought by the disabled person being discriminated against, or by the city attorney, district attorney, or Attorney General. [CC §§55; 55.1]

A property owner unlawfully discriminating against a disabled person is also liable for the disabled person's money losses caused by the unlawful refusal to rent. In addition to the disabled person's actual money losses, treble the amount of actual money losses may be awarded as punitive damages, plus attorney fees. The **minimum** monetary award for discrimination against a disabled person is $1,000. [CC §54.3]

This chapter presents California's enforcement of racial and familial discrimination rules in housing accommodations.

Discriminatory practices, exemptions and remedies

A minority tenant seeks to rent an apartment. The landlord states he will not rent an apartment to a tenant until a credit check has been completed. The landlord declines to accept a deposit from the tenant until his credit has been cleared.

Later the same day, a non-minority tenant seeks to rent the same apartment. The landlord agrees to rent the apartment to the non-minority tenant without first requiring a credit check. The landlord immediately accepts a check from the tenant as a deposit on the apartment.

The minority tenant is then informed the apartment has been rented to another person.

The minority tenant files a complaint against the landlord, claiming the landlord discriminated against him by refusing to rent an apartment to him based on his race. The landlord claims no discrimination occurred since he is entitled to require a credit check of prospective tenants.

However, requiring a credit check of minority tenants, but not non-minority tenants, is an unlawful discriminatory practice. The minority tenant is entitled to an award for money damages against the landlord. [**Stearns** v. **Fair Employment Practice Commission** (1971) 6 C3d 205]

Prohibited factors

California law prohibits discrimination in the sale or rental of housing accommodations based on the distinguishing factors of race, color, religion, sex, marital status, national origin, ancestry, familial status or disability.

Discriminatory practices include:

- *making an inquiry*, written or oral, into the race, sex, disability, etc. of any person seeking to rent or purchase housing;

- ads or notices for the sale or the rental of housing which *indicate a preference* or limitation based on any of the prohibited factors;

- *use of prohibited discrimination* when providing or arranging real estate loans and financing;

- *refusal based on a prohibited factor* by a broker to represent an individual in a real estate transaction; and

- any other practice that denies housing to a member of a protected class. [Calif. Government Code §12955]

Familial status in anti-discrimination law refers to a situation in which children under the age of 18 live with a parent or guardian. [Gov C §12955.2]

Until familial status was added to the anti-discrimination laws in 1992, it was legal to exclude minors under the age of 18 from housing accommodations. However, policies excluding children under the age of 18 are now classified as unlawful discrimination, unless the property qualifies as senior citizen housing. [Gov C §12955.9]

As with senior citizen housing, an exemption also exists for religious groups. Religious organizations may *give preference* to members of the same religious group when providing residential property for noncommercial purposes. [Gov C §12955.4]

However, a landlord may not use religious beliefs to shield discriminatory conduct.

For example, a landlord, for religious reasons, refuses to rent an apartment to an unmarried couple.

The couple files a complaint with the housing commission, and the commission rules the landlord violated fair housing laws which prohibit discrimination based on marital status.

The landlord claims refusing to rent to an unmarried couple is not discriminatory since renting to the unmarried couple would violate his religious beliefs regarding cohabitation of unmarried couples.

Can the landlord refuse to rent to the couple based on their marital status?

No! The landlord's refusal to rent to unmarried couples violates fair housing laws since the landlord's religious beliefs do not require him to participate in the business of renting property, and the fair housing law prohibiting discrimination based on marital beliefs does not interfere with the practice of his religion. [**Smith** v. **Fair Employment and Housing Commission** (1996) 12 C4th 1143]

Enforcement

The Department of Fair Employment and Housing (Department) and the Fair Employment and Housing Commission (Commission) are the agencies of the California state government which enforce anti-discrimination law. [Gov C §§12901; 12903; 12930; 12935]

Any person who feels they have been discriminated against may bring a complaint to the Department of Fair Employment and Housing. The Department investigates the complaint and seeks to resolve the situation through discussions with the person against whom the complaint is made. [Gov C §12980]

If the Department believes a discriminatory practice has occurred and is unable to reach a resolution through informal discussions, the Department then submits an *accusation* to the Fair Employment and Housing Commission. [Gov C §12981]

The Commission holds a hearing on the accusation. If the Commission finds unlawful discrimination has occurred, it may order a remedy for the person complaining of discrimination, such as ordering the person accused of discrimination to sell or rent property to the person bringing the complaint. The Commission may also impose punitive damages of up to $10,000. [Gov C §12987]

For example, an unmarried couple seeks to rent an apartment. Both agree to sign the lease agreement. The landlord discovers the couple is unmarried, and refuses to rent the apartment to the couple.

The unmarried couple files a complaint with the Department of Fair Employment and Housing, claiming the landlord's refusal to rent the apartment to them based on their marital status is unlawful discrimination.

The landlord claims his refusal to rent an apartment to the unmarried couple is based on legitimate business considerations, since unmarried couples are not liable for each other's debts as are married couples.

The couple claim their unmarried status does not expose the landlord to greater financial risk since each would be liable for the full amount of the rent under a lease agreement signed by both of them.

The Department is unable to resolve the dispute, and a formal accusation is submitted to the Fair Employment and Housing Commission.

The Commission finds the landlord discriminated against the couple since no legitimate business interest existed which justified the landlord's refusal to rent to the couple. The Commission awards the couple $2,000 in punitive damages. [**Hess** v. **Fair Employment and Housing Commission** (1982) 138 CA3d 232]

Chapter 7

DRE regulation of discrimination

This chapter presents discrimination activities of licensees while acting as agents.

Guidelines for broker conduct

Several regulations prohibiting discriminatory practices by real estate brokers have been established by the Department of Real Estate (DRE). A broker found guilty of engaging in discriminatory business practices may be disciplined by the DRE. [Department of Real Estate Regulation §2780]

Prohibited discriminatory practices include any situation in which a broker, while acting as an agent, discriminates against anyone based on race, color, sex, religion, ancestry, disability, marital status or national origin. Discriminary practices include:

- refusing to negotiate for the purchase, sale or rental of real estate;

- refusing to show property or provide information, or steering clients away from specific properties;

- discriminating in the terms and conditions of a real estate sale, such as charging minority buyers higher prices;

- refusing to accept a rental or sales listing or an application for financing;

- publishing or distributing advertisements which indicate a discriminatory preference;

- limiting access to Multiple Listing Services (MLS);

- any discrimination in the course of providing property management services;

- agreeing with a client to discriminate when selling or leasing the client's property, such as agreeing not to show the property to members of particular minority groups;

- attempting to discourage the purchase or rental of real estate based on representations of the race, sex, disability, etc. of other inhabitants in an area; and

- encouraging or permitting employees to engage in discriminatory practices.

For example, a broker is aware a licensed care facility for disabled people is located in a single-family residence near a residence his client is interested in buying.

The presence of the facility might influence the client's decision to purchase the property. However, to volunteer information to the client about the facility — rather than on inquiry from the buyer — would be unlawful discrimination. The broker may not attempt to influence the buyer's decision based on representations of the disability of other inhabitants in the area. [73 Ops. Cal. Atty. Gen. 58 (1990)]

Blockbusting

Regulations also prohibit the old practice of blockbusting, also known as *panic selling*. [DRE Reg. §2781]

Panic selling is an attempt to influence sales or rentals of real estate through representations about a change in the ethnic makeup of a neighborhood and the consequences of the economic impact brought about by the change. [See Chapter 1]

Of course, such blatantly discriminatory practices are not as common now as they once were. The focus now is on *implicit discrimination* — practices which are not openly discriminatory, but which have discriminatory effects.

Broker's duty to employees

A broker has a duty to advise his agents and employees of anti-discrimination rules, including DRE regulations, the *Unruh Civil Rights Act*, the *Fair Employment and Housing Act*, and federal fair housing law. [DRE Reg. §2725(f)]

Thus, the broker is not only responsible for his own conduct, but must also take steps to ensure his employees follow anti-discrimination regulations when acting as agents on his behalf.

Chapter 8

Equal Credit Opportunity Act

This chapter presents the federal rules which require those who make or arrange loans to eliminate discriminatory practices.

Federal fair lending rules

An unmarried couple applies for a home loan which will be evidenced by a note and trust deed signed by both ·of them. The couple fills out an application stating their separate incomes which, when combined, are sufficient to qualify for the loan. The lender conducts a credit check and denies the loan.

The lender informs the couple their loan application has been denied since they are not married and their separate incomes are not sufficient to allow each of them to independently qualify for the loan. The lender will not allow them to rely on each other's income to qualify. The couple is unable to locate another lender before their purchase agreement is cancelled by the seller.

The couple seeks to recover their losses from the lender under the federal *Equal Credit Opportunity Act*, claiming the lender has unlawfully discriminated against them based on their marital status.

The lender claims the denial of the loan to the unmarried couple is motivated by a legitimate business consideration since the couple's separate incomes are not sufficient to cover the loan, and unmarried couples are not liable for each other's debts, as are married couples.

However, the lender has no valid reason not to consider the couple's combined income in determining whether their income is sufficient to qualify for the loan since both will sign the note and **both will be liable** for the loan. Thus, the lender's denial of the couple's loan application is based on their marital status, a form of unlawful discrimination. [**Markham** v. **Colonial Mortgage Service Co. Associates, Inc.** (1979) 605 F2d 566]

Fairness in lending

The *Equal Credit Opportunity Act* prohibits discrimination in lending based on race, color, religion, national origin, sex, marital status or age (provided an individual is of legal age).

The anti-discrimination rules apply to institutional lenders, loan brokers, and others who regularly **make or arrange loans**. [15 United States Code §1691a(e)]

Income from a public assistance program, such as **welfare or social security**, must be considered by lenders and loan brokers as part of an applicant's income. To deny a loan based on an applicant's receipt of income from a public assistance program is unlawful discrimination. [15 USC §1691(a)(2)]

Discriminatory practices take many forms, including:

- treating minority loan applicants less favorably than non-minority applicants, or placing additional burdens on minority applicants;

- requiring a spouse's signature on a loan application when an applicant qualifies for a loan individually [**Anderson** v. **United Finance Company** (1982) 666 F2d 1274];

- discouraging loan applicants based on their race, color, sex, etc. [12 Code of Federal Regulations §202.5(a)]; and

- making inquiries into the race, sex, etc. of loan applicants. [12 CFR §202.5(d)]

Also, the lender may not make any inquiries into whether a loan applicant's income is derived from **alimony or child support**, or whether the applicant intends to bear children. [12 CFR §202.5(d)]

However, discrimination is rarely practiced overtly. Most lenders are not transparent enough for the consumer to see the discrimination. Most often, discrimination takes the form of a lender denying a loan to a minority borrower without a valid reason, or applying different standards to minority and non-minority borrowers.

Also, lenders and brokers must be careful not to provide more assistance to non-minority borrowers than to minority borrowers when preparing applications and working out problems which arise. The **different treatment** of minority and non-minority applicants is another form of unlawful discrimination.

For example, an African-American couple applies for a loan insured by the Federal Housing Administration (FHA) to purchase a residence. The home the couple seeks to purchase is 75 miles from their place of work. The couple intends to occupy the home as their principal residence and commute to work.

The lender suspects the couple wants to purchase the home as an investment, and not to occupy it themselves. Since FHA loans may only be used to purchase homes which the buyer will occupy, the lender denies the loan application.

The lender does not discuss with the couple whether they intend to occupy the home. Also, the lender never suggests the couple can apply for a non-FHA loan. Due to a loan contingency, the couple loses the right to buy the home.

The couple then seeks to recover their money losses from the lender under the *Equal Credit Opportunity Act*, claiming the lender's denial of their loan application was due to unlawful discrimination based on their race.

The lender claims the denial of the loan application was proper since it believed the couple did not intend to occupy the home, and thus did not qualify for an FHA loan.

However, the lender may not unilaterally decide the couple did not intend to occupy the home without first discussing the couple's intentions with them. Also, even if the couple did not qualify for an FHA loan, the lender could have assisted them with or referred them to other forms of financing.

Thus, the lender has discriminated against the African-American couple by denying their loan application without a valid reason, and failing to use diligence in assisting the couple in obtaining other financing. [**Barber** v. **Rancho Mortgage & Investment Corp.** (1994) 26 CA4th 1819]

Discrimination by age

Some exceptions to the anti-discrimination rules do exist.

For example, a lender may lawfully consider a loan applicant's age and whether the applicant receives income from a public assistance program when determining the applicant's creditworthiness. [15 USC §1691(b)(2)]

Editor's note — Allowing lenders to consider an applicant's age or receipt of income from a public assistance program as an exception in determining the applicant's creditworthiness effectively removes these two factors from the anti-discrimination protection previously discussed.

While a lender may not refuse to accept applications or impose different loan terms based on an applicant's age or receipt of public assistance income, the lender can lawfully deny a loan based on these factors simply by stating the applicant is not creditworthy.

Also, lenders may consider an applicant's **immigration status** when considering loan applications to determine whether the applicant is a permanent resident of the United States. [12 CFR §202.6(b)(7)]

After the lender's receipt of a loan application, the lender has 30 days to notify the applicant as to whether the loan is approved or denied. If the lender denies the loan application, the lender must deliver a statement to the applicant listing the specific reasons for the denial. [15 USC §1691(d)]

Alternatively, if the lender does not give the applicant a statement of the specific reasons for the denial, the lender must deliver a notice to the applicant that states the applicant has the right, upon request, to obtain a statement which lists the reasons for denial.

In addition to the *Equal Credit Opportunity Act*, California law controls credit reporting agencies. California grants consumers the right to inspect their files at any credit reporting agency. [Calif. Civil Code §1785.10]

Also, like the federal law, California law requires lenders using credit reporting services to provide loan applicants a statement of reasons if their loan application is denied. [CC §1785.20]

Penalties for discrimination in lending include actual money losses sustained by a person who has been discriminated against and punitive money awards of up to $10,000, plus attorney fees. [15 USC §1691e]

Chapter 9

The Housing Financial Discrimination Act of 1977

This chapter reviews a creditworthy individual's entitlement to a loan secured by a fairly appraised home.

California's fair lending laws

To achieve a healthy state economy, all residential housing placed on the real estate market for sale must be available to any homebuyer who is creditworthy and qualifies for purchase-assist financing. [Calif. Health and Safety Code §35801(b),(c)]

Also, an efficient real estate market requires the value of housing to not be susceptible to fluctuations caused by lenders who arbitrarily deny equity financing to qualified homeowners.

Thus, state law prohibits discriminatory lending practices. The goal of anti-discrimination law in home financing is to:

- increase the amount of housing available to creditworthy buyers; and

- increase lending in communities where lenders have made conventional home loans unavailable. [Health & S C §35802]

Increased availability of home loans

Lenders must make financing available to all qualified creditworthy loan applicants attempting to acquire loans to:

- buy, build, repair, improve or refinance an existing loan on a one-to-four unit, owner-occupied residence; or

- improve one-to-four unit residences which are not owner-occupied. [Health & S C §35805(d)]

Lenders violate public policy when they indicate a **discriminatory preference** by denying or approving financing to creditworthy home loan applicants based on the applicant's:

- race;

- color;

- religion;

- sex;

- marital status;

- national origin; or

- ancestry. [Health & S C §35811]

In a community which is composed mainly of residents of a certain race, color, religion or other minority status protected by law, a lender cannot:

- refuse to fund a home loan to a creditworthy buyer based on the demographics of that community; or

- appraise real estate in that community at a lower value than comparable real estate in communities predominantly composed of non-minority residents. [Health & S C §§35810; 35812]

Failing to provide financing in certain communities, called *redlining*, is specifically targeted for correction by the law since the failure to lend adversely affects the health, welfare and safety of California residents. [Health & S C §35801(e)(4)]

Lenders who deny loan applications, based on the characteristics of the community where the real estate offered as security is located, discourage homeownership in the community. Thus, redlining leads to a decline in the quality and quantity of housing in areas where financing is generally unavailable. [Health & S C §35801]

However, a lender can consider neighborhood conditions when making a loan. When doing so, the lender must demonstrate a denial based on neighborhood conditions is necessary to avoid an unsafe and unsound loan as a matter of good business practice. [Health & S C §35810]

For example, a lender is not precluded from considering the fair market value of real estate intended to secure a home loan. A property appraisal, however, cannot be based in any part on the demographic makeup of the area where the real estate is located.

Also, if the property's topography, structure or location is unsafe or unhealthy for a prospective occupant, the lender is not required to provide purchase-assist financing. [Health & S C §35813]

Notice of loan applicant's rights

Lenders are required to post in a conspicuous public location at their place of business a written notice in no less than 10-point type informing applicants for loans to be secured by an owner-occupied, one-to-four unit residential property of:

- their right to file a lending discrimination claim; and

- the name and address of the Secretary of the California Business, Transportation and Housing Agency (Housing). [Health & S C §35830]

Lenders subject to this posting requirement include **state regulated** banks, thrifts, public agencies or other institutions which make, arrange or buy loans funded to buy, build, repair, improve or refinance one-to-four unit, owner-occupied housing. [Health & S C §35805]

A home loan applicant who believes he has been unfairly discriminated against by a state lending institution must exhaust the Housing Agency's administrative remedies before suing the lender for money losses.

However, federally regulated banks and thrifts are not subject to state regulation and discipline. [**Conference of Federal Savings and Loans Associations** v. **Stein** (1979) 604 F2d 1256]

Administrative remedies

A loan applicant may file a discrimination claim with the California Secretary of Business, Transportation and Housing Agency against a state regulated lender if the applicant believes his loan application was denied due to:

- his race, color, religion, sex, marital status, national origin or ancestry; or

- trends, conditions or characteristics of the community where the real estate which will secure the loan is located. [Health & S C §35800 et seq.]

Once the claim is received, the Secretary will attempt to work with the lender to end any unlawful discriminatory lending practices. [Health & S C §35821]

If, within 30 days of receiving the complaint, the Secretary determines the lender has engaged in an unlawful discriminatory practice, the Secretary will serve the lender with his written decision and an order requiring the lender to end the unlawful discriminatory practice. [Health & S C §35822]

The order will also require the lender to pay damages in an amount no greater than $1,000, unless it is still feasible for the lender to review the loan application under nondiscriminatory terms and provide the denied financing. [Health & S C §35822(a),(b)]

Lender liability

A minority buyer of real estate submits a loan application to a mortgage broker for a purchase-assist loan.

The mortgage broker fails to take the necessary steps to arrange a loan for the minority buyer, and denies the application. Concurrently, the mortgage broker makes or arranges similar financing for a non-minority buyer whose credit record is equivalent to or less worthy than the minority buyer.

The minority buyer seeks money damages from the mortgage broker for race discrimination.

The minority buyer claims the mortgage broker's denial of his loan application is discriminatory since the mortgage broker arranged loans for less qualified non-minority buyers.

The mortgage broker claims he did not discriminate against the minority buyer since the buyer did not qualify for the loan.

Is the mortgage broker liable for money damages for discrimination?

Yes! The mortgage broker's failure to arrange a loan for the minority buyer, while at the same time arranging loans for less qualified non-minority buyers, is discriminatory. [**Green** v. **Rancho Santa Margarita Mortgage Company** (1994) 28 CA4th 686]

Also, consider a California-regulated institutional lender or loan broker who regularly arranges alternative forms of financing with a variety of lenders. The lender or broker consistently informs non-minority loan applicants of their financing options when they deny a loan application.

The lender's or loan broker's failure to diligently provide the same forms of financing and assistance for minority loan applicants subjects the lender and the loan broker to liability for the minority applicant's money losses caused by the discrimination — the selective release of information based on status. [**Barber** v. **Rancho Mortgage & Investment Corp.** (1994) 26 CA4th 1819]

Chapter 10

Home Mortgage Disclosure Act

This chapter discusses the prevention of lender discrimination under federal law.

Lenders release home loan data

The federal *Home Mortgage Disclosure Act (HMDA)* seeks to prevent lending discrimination and unlawful *redlining practices* on residential loans or home improvement loans by requiring lenders to disclose home loan origination information to the public. [Department of Housing and Urban Development Mortgagee Letter 94-22]

State and federally regulated banks, and persons engaged in the business of making home loans for profit, are required by the HMDA to compile home loan origination data for submission to their respective supervisory agencies. [12 United States Code §§2802; 2803; Calif. Health and Safety Code §35816]

Completed loan applications and loan originations to finance the purchase, construction, improvement of the loan applicant's home or to refinance an existing home loan are considered home loan originations. [12 USC §2803(a)]

Federal disclosure requirements

For lenders with total assets of more than $28 million and for-profit mortgage lenders with total assets of more than $10 million, the lender is required to compile data and make it available to the public. The data will include:

- the type and purpose of the loan;

- the owner-occupancy status of the real estate securing the loan;

- the amount of the loan;

- the action taken by the lender on the application;

- the sex and race or national origin of the loan applicant; and

- the income of the loan applicant. [12 Code of Federal Regulations §203.4(a)]

The data is then grouped according to census tracts to determine the lender's activity with the tract. [12 USC §2803(j)(2)(C)]

However, lenders are exempt from HMDA disclosure requirements if:

- the lender does not have a branch office in a metropolitan statistical area (MSA);

- the lender's assets on the preceding December 31 totalled less than $28 million. [12 CFR §203.3(a)(1)]

For-profit mortgage lenders are exempt from HMDA disclosure requirements if on the preceding December 31:

- the mortgage lender did not have a branch office in a MSA; or

- the mortgage lender's assets totalled less than $10 million and the lender originated less than 100 home purchase loans in the preceding year. [12 CFR §203.3(a)(2)]

Regardless of exemptions, all lenders approved by the Department of Housing and Urban Development (HUD) must report to HUD and disclose the census tract information on all Federal Housing Administration (FHA) loans they originate. [HUD Mortgagee Letter 94-22]

The data is then compiled by the Federal Financial Institutions Council into a **disclosure statement** which is sent to the lender. [12 CFR §203.5(b)]

The disclosure statement must be posted in a conspicuous location in the lender's home office where it is readily accessible to the public. The disclosure must remain posted for five years. [12 USC §2803(a)(2),(b),(c)]

On request from a broker, or any other member of the public, the lender must make available a copy of the disclosure statement data. [12 USC §2803(a)(1)]

California state regulated lenders

Lenders who regularly originate residential loans and do not report to a federal or state regulatory agency are required to compile data on the number and dollar amount of loan originations — actual originations and completed loan applications — for each fiscal year. [21 Calif. Code of Regulations §7118(a)]

Examples of state regulated lenders who fall into this category include insurers, mortgage bankers, investment bankers and credit unions that do not make federally related mortgage loans.

The data is first categorized by geographical area, then by census tract. For each census tract, loan originations are grouped according to:

- FHA, FmHA and Veterans Administration (VA) loan originations on owner-occupied, one-to-four unit dwellings;

- conventional purchase-assist loan originations on owner-occupied, one-to-four unit dwellings;

- home improvement loan originations on owner-occupied, one-to-four unit dwellings; and

- home improvement loan originations on occupied, one-to-four unit dwellings not occupied by the owner. [21 CCR §7118(b)(2)]

California regulated lenders exempt from loan origination disclosures are:

- lenders whose originations of purchase-assist loans totalled less than 10% of the lender's loan volume during the current reporting year; and

- licensed real estate brokers who negotiate or arrange purchase-assist and home improvement loans. [21 CCR §7121]

Monitoring federally regulated lenders

Federally regulated lenders are subject to investigation and penalties by federal authorities. [12 USC §2803(h)]

While disclosure of home loan statistics helps to identify lending patterns, loan statistics alone are not sufficient to determine whether a lender is unlawfully practicing redlining or discrimination.

The loan statistic disclosures may be relevant when considered in conjunction with other evidence, such as the credit histories of denied loan applicants and debt ratios. [HUD Mortgagee Letter 94-22]

Monitoring lending patterns of state lenders

The California Secretary of the Business, Transportation and Housing Agency monitors the practices and patterns of state regulated lenders to identify lenders whose lending practices warrant further investigation. The patterns of loan originations for loans secured by all types of real estate are monitored. [Health & S C §35815]

If the lender is licensed under a state agency, the state licensing agency monitors the lender for redlining and discrimination violations. [Health & S C §35814]

For example, mortgage bankers and lenders who use their real estate license to arrange loans are monitored by the Department of Real Estate (DRE). [21 CCR §7117(b)(1)]

The state secretary or agency monitoring a lender can enforce compliance with anti-redlining and anti-discrimination laws by imposing penalties, including a recommendation to the state treasurer not to deposit state funds with a lender who is in violation of the law. [Health & S C §35815(a)]

Chapter 11

HUD advertising guidelines for sales and rentals

This chapter reviews the advertising guidelines for the sale and rental of residential property established by the Department of Housing and Urban Development (HUD).

Avoiding discrimination in advertising

The printing or publishing of an advertisement for the sale or rental of buildings designed for residential occupancy, called *dwellings*, that indicates a *discriminatory preference*, is a violation of the *Federal Fair Housing Act (FFHA)*. [42 United States Code §3604(c); See Chapter 1]

The discriminatory preference rule applies to all brokers, developers and landlords in the business of selling or renting dwellings. [42 USC §§3603; 3604]

Real estate advertising guidelines are issued by the Department of Housing and Urban Development (HUD). The guidelines are the criteria by which the HUD Assistant Secretary for Fair Housing and Equal Opportunity determines whether a broker has practiced or will practice discriminatory preferences in their advertising and availability of real estate services.

However, HUD guidelines also help the broker, developer, and landlord avoid signalling preferences or limitations for any group of persons when marketing real estate for sale or rent.

Marketing real estate for sale or rent

The selective use of words, phrases, symbols, visual aids and media in the advertising of real estate may indicate a discriminatory preference held by the advertiser. When published, the preference could lead to a claim of discriminatory housing practices.

Words in a broker's real estate advertisement that indicate a particular race, color, sex, handicap, familial status or national origin are considered likely violations of the FFHA.

A broker should be aware of and refuse to use phrases that indicate a preference, even if requested by a seller or landlord, such as:

- white private home;

- Jewish home;

- black home; or

- adult building.

Catch words which may convey discriminatory preferences and are often used in a discriminatory context should also be avoided. Preferences are often voiced in colloquialisms and words such as *restricted, exclusive, private, integrated* or *membership approval*.

Indicating a preference by age is an *exclusion* from unlawful discrimination when marketing qualified 55-or-over residences or communities. [See Chapter 4]

Selective use of *media* or *human models* in an advertising campaign can also lead to discrimination against minority groups.

For example, a broker works in a metropolitan area and markets single-family residences (SFRs). A significant number of people residing in the area speak a language other than English.

Although several non-English publications are printed in the area, the broker advertises the residences only in publications printed in English. Also, the broker distributes fliers only in neighborhoods where the majority of the residents speak English.

Since the residence is advertised exclusively in English language media and the broker has limited his advertising to English speaking communities, the broker may be construed as indicating a discriminatory preference for English speaking buyers.

The HUD fair housing poster

The Department of Housing and Urban Development (HUD) issues guidelines that require real estate brokers marketing dwellings to display a *fair housing poster*. [24 CFR §§110.1; 110.10]

The fair housing poster is available at any HUD office. [24 CFR §110.20]

The broker marketing dwellings for sale or rent is to display the fair housing poster:

- in the broker's place of business; and

- at any dwelling offered for sale, other than SFRs. [24 CFR §110.10(a)]

Thus, a broker holding an open house at a SFR listed for resale is not required to display the fair housing poster at the residence.

However, if the dwellings marketed are part of a residential development, the fair housing poster must also be displayed by the developer during construction of the development. Later, the poster is to be displayed in the model dwellings whether or not the dwellings are sold employing a broker's services. [24 CFR §110.10(a)(2)(ii),(3)]

The fair housing posters must be placed where they can be easily seen by any persons seeking to:

- engage the services of the broker to list or locate a dwelling; or

- purchase a dwelling in a residential development. [24 CFR §110.15]

Failure to follow HUD guidelines

Even though required, a broker will not be subject to any penalties for failing to display the fair housing poster. However, failure to display the fair housing poster is initially considered sufficient evidence in a lawsuit to show that a broker practiced discriminatory housing practices. [24 CFR §110.30]

A real estate broker who follows HUD advertisement guidelines and displays the fair housing poster is less likely to practice a discriminatory activity. The fair housing poster assures potential sellers/landlords and buyers/tenants the broker does not unlawfully discriminate in the services he offers.

Also, the broker following HUD advertising and poster guidelines is in a better **position to defend** himself against a fair housing lawsuit.

Complying with HUD guidelines better assists the real estate broker to avoid prima facie violations of fair housing laws.

Use of the fair housing poster indicates to the public the broker's invitation to work with all individuals.

Chapter 12

AIDS and death disclosures

This chapter discusses the duty to disclose to residential buyers a prior occupant's death on the property.

No duty to disclose

A broker locates real estate for a buyer. The prior occupant of the property was infected with the Human Immundeficientcy Virus (HIV), the virus which causes Acquired Immune Deficiency Syndrome (AIDS).

Neither the broker nor the seller disclose their knowledge about the prior occupant's HIV-positive status. The buyer does not inquire about the health of the prior occupants.

The buyer purchases the property. Later, the buyer discovers the prior occupant was HIV-positive while residing on the property. The buyer immediately vacates the property and resells it at a loss.

The buyer seeks to recover his resale and relocation losses from the broker, claiming the broker had a duty to disclose his knowledge that the prior occupant was HIV-positive.

However, the buyer cannot recover his losses from the broker since a broker has no duty to disclose any prior occupant was infected with the HIV virus or afflicted with AIDS. [Calif. Civil Code §1710.2(a)]

On the sale or rental of a parcel of real estate or the transfer of any interest in the real estate, a broker has no affirmative duty to voluntarily disclose information regarding a prior occupant:

- infected with the HIV virus; or

- whose death, from any cause, occurred on the property more than three years prior to the purchase offer or rental agreement.

Further, California public policy prohibits a broker from disclosing a prior occupant's affliction with AIDS, even on the buyer's inquiry.

Also, individuals with the HIV virus are considered handicapped and are protected by the federal fair housing laws. [24 Code of Federal Regulations §100.201; See Chapter 1]

Disclosing death from AIDS

Unless the buyer makes a direct inquiry, the broker's affirmative duty to disclose material facts to the buyer in a sales transaction does not extend to the death of a prior occupant which occurred **more than three years** before the sale or lease of a property.

Consider a buyer who asks his broker if any AIDS-related deaths have occurred on the property.

On direct inquiry, the broker must disclose his knowledge of the facts concerning a death on the real estate. [CC §1710.2(d)]

If the broker is aware an AIDS-related death occurred on the property, he has a duty to disclose to the inquiring buyer:

- the prior occupant's death; and

- the death was AIDS-related.

If the broker has no knowledge of any AIDS-related deaths occurring on the property, he must disclose:

- his lack of such knowledge; and

- whether he intends to undertake an investigation to determine if an AIDS-related death occurred on the property.

However, consider a buyer's broker who is aware a death, from any cause including AIDS, occurred on the property within three years of his buyer's offer. The buyer does not inquire whether any deaths have occurred on the property.

Here, the broker needs to determine if a death on the property is a fact which will bear on the buyer's decision to purchase the property, called a *material fact*.

The broker should disclose any death occurring on the property within three years of his buyer's offer if he believes the death is a fact which will affect the buyer's decision to purchase the property.

TRUST FUNDS

Chapter 1

Trust funds overview

This chapter presents an insight into trust funds and their treatment.

Introduction to trust funds

In the course of his practice, a real estate licensee often finds himself in situations where he is handling other people's money. Funds belonging to others which a broker and his agents handle when acting as agents in a transaction are called *trust funds*. Trust funds include:

- rents and security deposits collected under a property management agreement;

- good faith deposits tendered by a buyer with an offer to purchase;

- fees and costs handed to the broker in advance of his or another's performance of agreed-to services; and

- loan payments and funds on contract collection and loan brokerage.

Trust funds must never be treated casually and without a sense of security for their safekeeping. State law and Department of Real Estate (DRE) regulations impose recordkeeping and accounting requirements on a broker's transfer or disbursement of trust funds.

The purpose of this reading material is to familiarize brokers with the requirements and procedures for the handling of trust funds. The writings presented here cover all trust fund aspects a real estate licensee needs to know, including:

- general laws and regulations defining and governing broker-held trust funds;

- special rules relating to the handling of advance fees and costs;

- how to open and operate a trust account; and

- recordkeeping and accounting procedures.

Identification of trust funds

Brokers, while acting in their capacity as agents in real estate transactions, receive funds to be **held in trust**. These funds, called *trust funds,* include:

- deposits on offers to purchase and applications to rent or borrow;

- fees advanced for any brokerage services to be provided in the future;

- funds advanced for future costs;

- funds from sellers, borrowers and landlords as reserves to cover future costs;

- rental income and tenant security deposits;

- funding for a loan or the purchase of real estate; and

- proceeds from a sale or financing.

Trust funds are received by a broker, or by an employee acting on behalf of the broker, as part of a transaction in which the broker is acting as an agent. Employees acting on behalf of a broker include sales agents, associated brokers, resident property managers and office personnel.

Trust funds include any *item or evidence of value* handed to the broker or the broker's employee while acting as an agent in a real estate transaction.

For example, a buyer enters into a purchase agreement. The buyer's good faith deposit is in the form of a bag of gems that is handed to the broker. The dollar value of the gems will apply toward the purchase price on closing.

Must the broker handle the bag of gems as trust funds?

Yes! All **items of value** received by the broker as part of a transaction for which a real estate license is required, regardless of form, are trust funds subject to special handling. Trust funds come in many forms, including checks, precious metals, coins or stamp collections, promissory notes, the pink slip to a car and any other item or evidence of value. [Calif. Business and Professions Code §10145]

Managing the trust funds

Now consider a broker who enters into a property management agreement with an owner of income-producing real estate. Management services to be performed by the broker under his license include locating tenants, collecting rent and deposits, and disbursing funds for payment of operating expenses and installments on a trust deed loan encumbering the real estate.

The broker is further authorized to withdraw his fee and send any funds remaining to the owner.

The broker takes possession of the property under the property management agreement.

The broker locates several new tenants and collects monthly rent and deposits.

The broker deposits the rent and security deposits he receives into his **general account**. He then enters the amount of each transaction as **trust funds** on the client's subaccount ledger.

Although sufficient funds are held in the client's subaccount to meet operating expenses and make the loan payment, the broker first withdraws his fee before making the loan payment authorized by the owner. The disbursement of the brokerage fee reduces the balance on the client's ledger below the amount needed to make the loan payment.

The broker then issues a check to the lender for the loan payment. The check bounces due to insufficient funds remaining in the broker's general account. The owner is notified by the lender and contacts the broker who provides funds to cover the loan payment.

However, when the rent and security deposits collected on behalf of his client were deposited into his general account rather than a trust account, the broker *illegally commingled* the owner's funds with his funds, even though a subaccount ledger for the client's trust funds was maintained.

Also, withdrawal of the brokerage fee before paying all other obligations the broker agreed to disburse on behalf of the owner, including payment on the loan, is a *conversion* of the client's funds to the broker's own use, a breach of the agency duties owed to the client. The brokerage/management fee is to be paid last, after agreed-to services have been performed, including all authorized disbursements.

Further, the broker misrepresented the availability of immediate funds, a fraud which is grounds for the revocation or suspension of his license, by writing a check for the loan payment when he knew insufficient funds existed in the account to cover the check. [**Apollo Estates, Inc.** v. **Department of Real Estate** (1985) 174 CA3d 625]

Consider a broker who maintains a brokerage trust account that holds loan payments received by the broker while servicing loans on behalf of trust deed investors.

The broker pledges the trust account to secure a personal loan from the same bank which holds the trust account.

The broker defaults on the loan, and the bank seizes the trust account funds.

An investor seeks to recover his trust account funds from the bank, claiming the bank's seizure of the funds is a *conversion* since trust funds cannot be taken to satisfy the broker's personal debt.

The bank claims the seizure of the trust account is not a conversion since it exercised its right to an offset under the security agreement.

Is the investor entitled to recover his portion of the trust funds?

Yes! The trust funds belong to the investor and must be returned. The bank's right to an offset for the broker's personal debt to the bank does not extend to seizure of funds held for others in the broker's trust account. [**Chazen** v. **Centennial Bank** (1998) 61 CA4th 532]

Handling cash and checks

Funds received in the form of cash or checks made payable to the broker while acting as an agent in a transaction are trust funds and must be:

- deposited into the broker's trust account;

- held undeposited as instructed; or

- endorsed and handed to others entitled to the funds.

Further, the broker has a duty to **secure trust funds** that are not in the form of cash or checks, such as gems, coins, notes or other personal property, from loss or damage after he receives them. Such nonnegotiable types of trust funds cannot be deposited in a bank account. Thus, the broker should place the nonnegotiable items in a safe or safe-deposit box for safekeeping until they are delivered to others.

Trust funds received in the form of checks or cash may only be used for expenditures authorized and incurred for the benefit of the owner of the funds.

Further, the broker must **regularly account** to the owner on the status, expenditure and location of the trust funds, called an *owner's statement*.

Prior to the end of the **third business day** following the day the broker receives trust funds in the form of cash or checks, the broker, unless instructed in writing to the contrary, must deposit the funds:

- with the **person or escrow** depository entitled to the funds (as payee or by endorsement); or

- in a **trust account** maintained by the broker at a bank or other state-recognized depository. [B & P C §10145; Department of Real Estate Regulation §2832(a)]

Also, when an agent of the broker accepts trust funds on behalf of the broker, the agent must immediately deliver the funds to the broker, unless directed by the broker to:

- deliver the trust funds to the person or the escrow entitled to the funds; or

- deposit the trust funds into the broker's trust account. [B & P C §10145(c)]

For example, when a broker negotiates the purchase or lease of real estate, he usually receives a check as a good faith deposit on an offer to purchase or lease.

The broker may hold the check undeposited until an event occurs, such as the offer is accepted or escrow is opened, if:

- the check is made payable to someone other than the broker; or

- the check is made payable to the broker with **written instructions**, typically from the buyer or tenant, to hold the check undeposited until acceptance of the offer or escrow is opened; **and**

- the person to whom the offer is submitted, usually the seller or landlord, is informed the check for the good faith deposit is being held by the broker when the offer is submitted. [DRE Reg. §2832(c)]

The instructions to hold the check undeposited until acceptance are included in the terms for receipt of the deposit contained in the offer to purchase or lease. [See **first tuesday** Form 150 §1]

Also, after a buyer's offer is accepted, the broker may continue to hold the buyer's check for the good faith money undeposited if the seller gives the broker written instructions to continue to hold the check undeposited.

However, without instructions to further retain the check undeposited, the broker must deposit or deliver the funds by the end of the **next business day** after acceptance:

- to the payee entitled to the funds, such as a title company or escrow;

- into the broker's trust account at a bank or other state-recognized depository, such as a thrift; or

- to an escrow depository on the broker's endorsement, if the broker is the payee and does not want to deposit and disburse from his trust account to escrow. [DRE Reg. §2832]

Identifying the owner

A broker must at all times know who owns and controls the funds held in his trust account. Trust funds can only be disbursed on the authorization of the owner of the funds. *Subaccount ledgers* are set up to identify the owner of funds and the amount held for the owner.

However, persons other than the owner of the trust funds may have an interest in the funds. If so, their authorization is also required to withdraw the funds.

For example, a buyer, as a good faith deposit on an offer to purchase, issues a check payable to a broker with instructions in the purchase agreement to hold the check undeposited until acceptance of the offer.

The seller accepts the buyer's offer and the broker deposits the check in his trust account as funds held on behalf of and owned by the buyer.

The buyer is unable to obtain a purchase-assist loan to fund the purchase. The buyer cancels the transaction, consistent with the loan contingency provision in the purchase agreement. However, the seller does not sign cancellation instructions or other instructions to authorize disbursement (return) of the buyer's deposit. [See **first tuesday** Form 183]

The buyer then makes an offer to purchase real estate owned by another seller, which is accepted.

To obtain funds to close escrow on the second transaction, the buyer makes a demand on the broker to transfer the buyer's good faith deposit on the first transaction from the trust account to the escrow handling the second transaction. The broker refuses to withdraw the buyer's good faith deposit from his trust account without further instructions from the seller under the purchase agreement cancelled by the buyer.

Did the broker act correctly when retaining the buyer's good faith deposit?

Yes! When a buyer's offer, which includes receipt of a good faith deposit, **is accepted** by a seller and the buyer's good faith deposit is placed in the broker's trust fund account (or the purchase escrow), the buyer's funds may not be withdrawn without written authorization signed by both the buyer and seller. If funds are disbursed without mutual instructions, the broker is liable to the seller for losses due to an improper release of the funds. [**Mullen** v. **Department of Real Estate** (1988) 204 CA3d 295]

Chapter 2

Advance fees as trust funds

This chapter discusses a broker's handling and accounting of advance fees.

Trust funds retain status after withdrawal

A broker is employed by a seller under an exclusive right-to-sell listing agreement. The listing calls for the broker to receive a percentage of the purchase price as his brokerage fee **on delivery** of a signed offer to purchase the property on terms stated in the listing agreement or accepted by the seller. [See **first tuesday** Form 102]

The broker locates a buyer who makes an offer to buy the real estate. The purchase agreement provides for the payment of the broker's fee at the close of escrow, not on acceptance as provided in the listing agreement.

As receipted and instructed in the purchase agreement, the buyer's check for good faith money, payable to the broker, is to be deposited on the acceptance of the offer. The offer is accepted and the broker deposits the check in his trust account.

Escrow is opened. The buyer and seller proceed to eliminate contingencies and prepare to close escrow.

The broker's fee on the transaction is less than the amount of the buyer's good faith deposit that is still held by the broker in his trust account. The broker, without authorization from the buyer and the seller, withdraws the amount of his brokerage fee from the trust account, payable to himself, before the close of escrow.

Can the broker advance to himself all or part of his fee by a withdrawal from the trust account prior to close of the sales escrow without further authority from the buyer and seller?

No! The broker is not entitled to payment of his brokerage fee on the transaction until the sale closes. The purchase agreement called for the fee to be paid on close of the sales transaction. The funds the broker withdrew from the trust account in advance of closing were still the buyer's funds controlled by the terms of the buyer's purchase agreement, not the seller's listing agreement with the broker. The premature withdrawal required signed authority from the buyer and the seller.

By withdrawing the buyer's funds, the broker unlawfully commingled trust funds with his other funds. [**Bell** v. **Watson** (1957) 148 CA2d 684]

Advance fee accounting

Brokerage fees deposited with the broker before they are earned, called *advance fees*, must be deposited in the broker's trust account. The funds belong to the broker's client, not the broker. Further, advance fees cannot be withdrawn by the broker before they are earned and a statement is sent to the client.

In addition to the regular trust fund accounting requirements a broker must follow when accepting **advance fees**, the broker must send the client a *verified copy* of the advance fee accounting no later than at the end of each calendar quarter, and at the time the contract between the broker and the client is completely performed.

The amounts placed in the trust account may be withdrawn when expended for the benefit of the client, or on the fifth day after the verified accounting is mailed to the client. [Calif. Business and Professions Code §10146]

The verified accounting for the advance fees must include:

- the name of the broker;

- the name of the client;

- a description of the services rendered or to be rendered;

- an identification of the trust fund account and where the advance fee is deposited; and

- the amount of the advance fee collected. [Department of Real Estate Regulation §2972]

In addition, the verified accounting must include the amount allocated to each of the following:

- providing the agreed-to services;

- commissions paid to field agents and representatives; and

- overhead costs and profits. [DRE Reg. §2972(f)]

If a disbursement from the account is made for advertisement, the verified accounting must include:

- a copy of the advertisement;

- the name of the publication in which the advertisement appeared; and

- the number of ads published and the dates they appeared. [DRE Reg. §2972(g)]

Also, if the advance fee is for the arrangement of a loan, the verified accounting must include a list of the names and addresses of the persons to whom the information pertaining to the loan requirements was submitted, and the dates the information was submitted. [DRE Reg. §2972(h)]

Approval of advance fee agreements

All solicitations, advertising and agreements used by a broker to obtain an advance fee from a client must be submitted to the Commissioner of the Department of Real Estate (DRE) for approval at least 10 calendar days prior to use. [DRE Reg. §2970]

If the Commissioner determines within 10 calendar days of receiving the material that the material would tend to mislead clients, the Commissioner may order the broker to refrain from using the material. [B & P C §10085]

To be approved by the Commissioner, the advance fee agreement and any materials to be used with the agreement must:

- contain the total amount of the advance fee and the date or event the fees will become due and payable as earned;

- list a specific and complete description of the services to be rendered to earn the advance fee;

- give a definite date for full performance of the services described in the advance fee agreement; and

- contain no false, misleading or deceptive representations. [DRE Reg. §2970(b); See **first tuesday** Form 106]

Also, the advance fee agreement may not contain:

- a provision relieving the broker from an obligation to perform verbal agreements made by his employees or agents [DRE Reg. §2970(b)(4),(5)]; nor

- a guarantee the transaction involved will be completed.

Chapter 3

Advance costs as trust funds

This chapter discusses a broker's handling and accounting of advance costs and how to prepare the listing package advance cost sheet for listing packages.

Advance costs are trust funds

Funds advanced by the client directly to the broker for costs the client agrees to pay belong to the client belong· to the client. Typically, the seller will need to incur costs for the reports on the property to properly market the property to prospective buyers.

On receipt of a deposit from the client for payment of costs, the broker must place the advance deposit in a trust account in the broker's name since they are trust funds payable to the broker. [Calif. Business and Professions Code §10146]

An advance cost sheet included as part of the listing package acknowledges the broker's receipt of any deposit towards costs and authorizes the broker to make disbursement from the funds as the itemized costs are incurred. [See Form 107 accompanying this chapter.]

When the listing terminates, the broker must return all remaining trust funds to the client. The broker *cannot* use trust funds to offset any fees the client may owe him.

A statement which accounts for all funds held in trust must be handed to the client at least every calendar quarter. However, a monthly accounting by way of a copy of the client's trust account ledger creates a better business relationship.

A final accounting must be made when the listing agreement expires. Again, if any funds remain in trust, they must be returned to the client with this accounting. [B & P C §10146]

The **statement of account** for the trust funds must include at least the following information:

- the amount of the deposit toward advance costs;

- the amount of each disbursement of funds from the trust account;

- an itemized description of the cost obligation paid on each disbursement;

- the current remaining balance of the advance cost deposit; and

- an attached copy of any advertisements paid from the advance cost deposit.

Lastly, the broker must keep all accounting records for at least three years, and make the records available to the Department of Real Estate (DRE) on request. [B & P C §10148]

A broker who fails to place those advance cost deposits payable to him in his trust account or who later fails to deliver proper trust account statements to his client is *presumed* guilty of embezzlement. [**Burch** v. **Argus Properties, Inc.** (1979) 92 CA3d 128]

LISTING PACKAGE COST SHEET
Due Diligence Checklist

DATE:_____, 20_____, at _____, California

Items left blank or unchecked are not applicable.

1. FACTS:

1.1 This is an addendum of same date to the following:

☐ Seller's Listing Agreement [**first tuesday** Form 102]

☐ Buyer's Listing Agreement [ft Form 103]

☐ Loan Broker Listing Agreement [ft Form 104]

☐ _____

1.2 Entered into by:

Broker: _____

Client: _____

For a period beginning on _____, 20_____ and terminating on _____, 20_____.

2. BROKER'S PERFORMANCE:

2.1 Broker is hereby authorized and instructed to incur on behalf of the client the following estimated costs:

a. Natural hazard disclosure report . . . . $_____

b. Local ordinance compliance certificate . . . . $_____

c. Structural pest control report, and ☐ clearance . . . . $_____

d. Smoke detector and water heater anchor installation . . . . $_____

e. Property (Home) inspection report . . . . $_____

f. Association documents charge . . . . $_____

g. Lead-based paint report . . . . $_____

h. Mello Roos assessment notice . . . . $_____

i. Listing (transaction) coordinator's fees . . . . $_____

j. Well water quality and quantity report . . . . $_____

k. Septic/sewer report . . . . $_____

l. Soil report . . . . $_____

m. Survey of property (civil engineer) . . . . $_____

n. Appraisal report . . . . $_____

o. Architectural (floor) plans . . . . $_____

p. Title report ☐ property profile, ☐ preliminary report, ☐ abstract . . . . . . $_____

q. MLS or market session input fee . . . . $_____

r. Sign deposit or purchase, installation and removal . . . . $_____

s. Advertising in newspapers, magazines, radio or television . . . . $_____

t. Information flyers and postage (handout or mailing) . . . . $_____

u. Open house — food and spirits . . . . $_____

v. Photos or video of the property . . . . $_____

w. Credit report on buyer . . . . $_____

y. Travel expenses . . . . $_____

x. _____ . . . . $_____

z. _____ . . . . $_____

2.2 **TOTAL ESTIMATED COSTS** . . . . $_____

3. PAYMENT OF COSTS:

3.1 ☐ Client to pay those costs estimated in this agreement and incurred by the broker on presentation of a billing.

3.2 Client herewith hands Broker a deposit of $_____ as an advance for the payment of costs incurred on behalf of the Client as estimated in this agreement.

3.3 ☐ Costs paid which were incurred under this addendum shall be credited towards any contingency fee earned by Broker upon closing a transaction which in the subject of the underlying listing agreement.

4. TRUST ACCOUNT: (To be filled out only if a deposit is entered at §3.2 above.)

4.1 Broker will place the advance cost deposit received under § 3.1 above into his trust account maintained with _____ at their _____ branch.

4.2 These amounts required to pay when due and satisfy the obligations incurred as agreed. Broker is authorized and instructed to disburse from the trust account deposit.

4.3 Within 10 days after each calendar ☐ month, or ☐ quarter, and upon termination of this agreement, Broker will deliver to Client a statement of account for all funds withdrawn from the advance cost deposit handed Broker under §3.2 above.

4.4 Each statement of account delivered by Broker shall include no less than the following information:

   a. The amount of the advance cost deposit received.

   b. The amount of funds disbursed from the advance cost deposit.

   c. An itemization and description of the obligation paid on each disbursement.

   d. The current remaining balance of the advance cost deposit.

   e. An attached copy of any advertisements paid from the advance cost deposit since the last recorded accounting.

   f. _____

4.5 On termination of this agreement, Broker will return to Client all remaining trust funds.

I agree to the terms stated above.	I agree to the terms stated above.
Date:_____, 20_____	Date:_____, 20_____
Broker: _____	Client: _____
By: _____	Client Signature: _____
	Client Signature: _____

For example, a borrower retains a broker to assist in locating a lender who will make a loan to finance the acquisition of real estate. The borrower and broker enter into an exclusive right-to-borrow listing agreement.

The listing agreement assures the broker he will receive a brokerage fee when the loan he was employed to negotiate is funded by the lender he locates. [See **first tuesday** Form 104]

The broker includes an **advance cost sheet** as an attachment to the listing. The advance cost sheet calls for the borrower to advance funds to cover itemized costs, such as appraisals and credit reports, which will be incurred by the broker while arranging a loan to be secured by the property the borrower seeks to buy. The advance costs are separate and unrelated to payment of the broker's fee.

The borrower issues a check payable to the broker for the amount of the costs he has agreed to cover.

Can the broker deposit into his general business account part or all of the funds advanced by the borrower to cover costs which he is to pay on behalf of the borrower.

No! Funds received by the broker to hold and use to pay costs to be incurred **in the future** on behalf of the borrower are *trust funds*. They are held to pay the agreed-to costs itemized in the advance cost sheet attached to the listing agreement.

As trust funds, they will be deposited by the broker in a *trust account* in the broker's name, as trustee, and separate from accounts established to hold the broker's personal or business funds. [B & P C §10145]

Analyzing the listing package advance cost sheet

The item listed on the advance cost sheet are not generally costs which are part of the broker's overhead incurred to maintain his brokerage office. The costs listed, if incurred, relate primarily to the condition of the property listed, marketed and sold. The costs listed are incurred to document the integrity of the client's property, not to pay for the services of the broker and the listing agent. Thus, the cost rightly should be paid by the client who owns the property, not borne by his representatives — the broker or listing agent.

Editor's note — Some brokers and agents are aware of other brokers who fail to ask their clients for authority to order reports before a prospective buyer is located. Knowing this failure by others brokers and fearing the loss of a listing should they ask the seller to advance the costs, these brokers and agents are reticent to ask sellers to spend money on property reports. These reluctant brokers and listing agents find it easier to advance the cost of these reports themselves in the hope the property will sell and they will receive a fee to cover their advance.

When filling out the advance cost sheet, the client is given choices as to when and how he will pay the costs of reports.

The client may agree to pay the charges directly to third party vendors when billed, in which case the broker coordinates the arrangements for payment with the vendors as agent of the client. While the client's check is payable to the vendor, not the broker, if it is handed to a listing agent for delivery to the vendor, the check constitutes *trust funds* received by the broker that require an entry in the trust fund ledger maintained by the broker.

On the other hand, the client may deposit the estimated cost of the reports with the broker, making the check payable to the broker, called *advance costs*. The broker would then pay the charges from funds held on deposit when billed by the reporting service.

Preparing the Listing Package Advance Cost Addendum

Identification: **Enter** the date and place the agreement is prepared. This date is the date used to reference the document.

1. **Facts:**

   1.1 *Agreement reference*: **Check** the appropriate box to indicate the agreement to which this addendum is attached.

   1.2 *Agreement identification*: **Enter** the names of the broker and client in the transaction. **Enter** the date the listing agreement referenced in §1.1 begins and the date the listing agreement ends.

2. **Broker's Performance**:

   2.1 *Cost estimate*: **Enter** the dollar amounts estimated to be incurred for each of the following:

      a. *Natural hazard disclosure report*:

      b. Local ordinance compliance certificate:

      c. Structural pest control report and clearance:

      d. Smoke detector and water heater installation:

      e. Home inspection report:

      f. Homeowner's association (HOA) charge:

      g. Lead-based paint:

      h. Mello-Roos assessment notice:

      i. Transaction coordinator's fee:

      j. Well water quality and quantity report:

      k. Septic or sewer report:

      l. Soil report:

      m. Property survey:

      n. appraisal report:

      o. Architectural plans:

      p. Title report, property profile, preliminary report or abstract:

      q. MLS or other fee:

      r. sign deposit or purchase:

      s. Advertising:

      t. Flyers and postage:

      u. Open house provisions:

      v. Photos or video of property:

      w. Credit reports:

      x. Travel expenses:

      y. Other:

      z. Other:

   2.2 *Total estimated costs*: **Add** the figures in §2.1a through §2.1z. **Enter** the total as the total estimated costs to be incurred and paid for out of the deposit for costs.

3. **Payment of costs**:

   3.1 *Client to pay*: **Check** the box if the client is to pay the costs listed in §2 directly to the vendor on presentation of vendor's billing.

3.2 *Deposit for payment*: **Enter** the dollar amount of the deposit handed to the broker as an advance by the client toward the cost itemized.

3.3 *Fees including costs*: **Check** the box if costs incurred under this agreement are to be applied toward any fee earned by the broker on closing of the transaction.

4. **Trust Account**: This section is to be filled out *only* if a deposit amount is entered in §3.2 above.

   4.1 *Deposit of trust funds*: **Enter** the name of the financial institution where the broker will deposit the funds received under §3.2. **Enter** the address of the financial institution.

   4.2 *Authorization to pay:* Broker is instructed to disburse funds to pay for costs incurred under the agreement

   4.3 *Periodic accounting*: **Check** the box to indicate whether the broker will deliver a monthly or quarterly accounting of the trust funds.

   4.4 *Trust fund accounting*: The periodic statement of account to be delivered to the client regarding the trust funds must contain the following:

   a. The amount of the advance cost deposit initially received by the broker.

   b. The amount of advance costs disbursed.

   c. An itemized description of each amount disbursed from the account.

   d. The current balance after all advance cost disbursements have been deducted.

   e. A copy of all advertisements paid for from advance costs since the last statement.

   f. **Enter** any additional information to be included on the statement.

   4.5 *Return of trust funds*: Once the advance cost agreement is terminated, the broker is to return all remaining trust funds to the client.

Signatures:

Broker: **Enter** the date the broker signs the agreement. **Enter** the broker's name or the name of the agent acting on behalf of the broker. **Obtain** the broker's or agent's signature.

Client: **Enter** the date the client signs the agreement. **Enter** the client's name. **Obtain** the client's signatures.

Chapter 4

Trust accounts

This chapter discusses the types of trust accounts and the maintenance of trust account integrity.

Trust account withdrawals

Checks or cash are occasionally **made payable** and handed to a real estate broker during the course of his acting as an agent in a transaction. These items are trust funds since they do not belong to the broker. Thus, checks payable to the broker and cash are received in "trust" by the broker and must be deposited by the broker (unless endorsed and handed to others as instructed) into a **non-interest bearing** trust account.

The trust account opened for the deposit of cash and items payable to the broker must be in the name of the broker, as trustee, at a bank or a state-recognized depository, such as a thrift. [Calif. Business and Professions Code §10145]

Once trust funds are placed in the broker's trust account, the trust funds may only be withdrawn or disbursed as authorized and instructed by the owner of the trust funds and any third party who has an interest in the funds, such as a seller who acquires an interest in the buyer's good faith deposit on acceptance of a purchase agreement offer. [B & P C §10145(a)(1)]

Withdrawals or disbursements from the trust account of an **individual broker** must be made under the signature of:

- the broker named as trustee on the account;

- a licensed broker or salesagent employed by the named broker under a broker-agent employment agreement [See **first tuesday** Form 505]; or

- an unlicensed employee of the named broker, provided the unlicensed employee is **bonded** for the total amount of the trust funds the employee can access. [Department of Real Estate Regulation §2834(a)]

When a person other than the broker named as trustee on the trust account is a signer and can withdraw or disburse funds from the trust account, the person must be authorized as a signer in a writing signed by the broker. This authority would either be included in an addendum to the employment agreement or in the agreement itself.

When the trust account is in the name of a **corporate broker** as trustee, withdrawals are made by:

- the designated officer (DO) who qualified the corporation as a licensed broker; or

- a licensed or unlicensed employee with the written authorization of the designated officer. [DRE Reg. §2834(b)]

Again, the authorization from the corporation should be made part of the employment agreement with each signatory. [See **first tuesday** Forms 505, 510 or 511]

However, a broker's written delegation to others who are signers on the trust account with the authority to draw checks does not relieve the individual broker or the designated officer of a corporate broker from liability for any loss or misuse of trust funds. [DRE Reg. §2834(c)]

The broker should consider requiring two signatures on trust account withdrawals to help prevent an improper withdrawal by an individual signer. An insurance policy for the brokerage business should also include coverage of employees who have direct or indirect access to trust funds.

Interest-bearing accounts

Trust funds may be placed in an **interest-bearing** account if requested by the owner of the funds and agreed to by the broker. However, the broker is under no obligation to comply with the owner's request if he notifies the owner of the trust funds that he will not place the trust funds in an interest-bearing account [B & P C §10145(e)]

If the broker agrees to comply with an owner's request to place his trust funds in an interest-bearing trust account:

- a separate trust account must be established solely to hold the owner's trust funds;

- the trust account must be in the name of the broker as trustee, with the owner named as the specified beneficiary;

- the trust account must be insured by the Federal Deposit Insurance Corporation (FDIC); and

- the broker and his agents cannot receive any interest earned by the trust account, even if agreed to by the owner of the trust funds. [B & P C §10145(d)]

Also, if trust funds are to be placed in an interest-bearing account, the broker must first disclose:

- how interest is calculated on the account;

- who will receive the interest;

- who will pay bank service charges; and

- any penalties or notice requirements for withdrawal. [B & P C §10145(d)(4); See **first tuesday** Form 535 accompanying this chapter]

Improper commingling

If a broker deposits trust funds into an account he uses to receive and disburse personal or business funds, the broker has *improperly commingled* funds. Conversely if the broker places or leaves his personal funds in a trust account, he has also improperly commingled funds. The broker has mixed the client's funds with his personal or business the funds. [**Stillman Pond, Inc.** v. **Watson** (1953) 115 CA2d 440]

Except to the extent authorized by the Department of Real Estate (DRE) regulations, commingling is improper.

A broker is permitted to *appropriately commingle* his personal or business funds with trust funds in only the following two situations authorized by the DRE:

1. The broker may maintain a deposit of up to $200 of his **own funds** in the trust account to cover bank service charges on the account; and

2. Fees or reimbursement for costs **due the broker** from trust funds may remain in the trust account for up to 25 days before disbursement to the broker. [DRE Reg. §2835]

INTEREST-BEARING TRUST ACCOUNT AGREEMENT

DATE: _____, 20_____, at _____, California

Items left blank or unchecked are not applicable.

This agreement regarding the handling of trust funds is between _____,
Broker, and the depositor of the funds _____, **Owner**.

1. Owner hearby requests the Broker to hold under this agreement those trust funds in the amount of $_____ handed to the Broker by the Owner on execution of this agreement.

   1.1 The funds are held in trust to be disbursed for the purpose of completing the Owner's performance under an agreement entitled _____, dated _____, 20_____, entered into by the Owner and _____.

2. Broker is hearby authorized and instructed to deposit the trust funds into an interest-bearing trust account with _____, **Depository**, being a bank, thrift, credit union or industrial loan company whose accounts are insured by the Federal Deposit Insurance Company (FDIC). The address of the branch or location of the depository is _____.

   2.1 The trust account to be in the name of the Broker, as trustee for ☐ Owner, or ☐ _____.

   2.2 All funds in the trust account to be covered by FDIC insurance or other insurance by an agency of the United States.

   2.3 The type of interest-bearing account to be ☐ passbook, or ☐ time certificate, or ☐ _____.

   2.4 The annual rate of interest accruing on the account to be _____%.

   2.5 Interest accruing on the deposit to be compounded ☐ daily, ☐ monthly, or ☐ quarterly.

   2.6 A service charge ☐ is, or ☐ is not, imposed on the account by the Depository. If a service charge is imposed, it is to be deducted and paid from interest accruing on the account.

   2.7 Interest earned on the trust funds is to be paid to ☐ Owner, or ☐ _____, on (event) _____.

      a. Under no circumstances may the interest be paid, directly or indirectly, to the broker or a licensed person employed by the Broker.

   2.8 Withdrawal of the trust funds from the account ☐ prior to _____ days after deposit with the depository, or ☐ without _____ days prior notice, shall subject the funds to a penalty of $_____ for early withdrawal.

3. The trust account shall hold no other funds belonging to the Broker or held by the Broker for others as trust funds.

4. The trust account number is:_____

   4.1 Broker is authorized and instructed to enter the account number on this agreement when it is known to the Broker, and notify the Owner and other party named at §2.7 of the account number by promptly handing them a copy of this agreement containing the account number or sending a copy by regular USPS mail service.

5. Should these trust funds accepted by the Broker be for use in a real estate related transaction (purchase, lease, or loan), the other parties to the contract must consent to this agreement by signing the third party approval provision below.

I agree to the terms stated above.

Date:_____, 20_____

Broker:_____

Agent:_____

Signature:_____

I agree to the terms stated above.

Date:_____, 20_____

Owner's name:_____

Social Security #:_____

Signature:_____

I have read and approve this agreement.

Date:_____, 20_____

Third party's name:_____

Signature:_____

The improper commingling of trust funds and personal or business funds exposes the broker to revocation or suspension of his license. [B & P C §10176(e)]

For example, a broker prepares a purchase agreement offer for a buyer which includes the broker's receipt of a check for the buyer's good faith deposit. Instructions are not included in the purchase agreement authorizing the broker to hold the check undeposited until acceptance of the offer. [See **first tuesday** Forms 150 to 159]

The buyer signs the offer and issues a check payable to the broker for the good faith deposit. The broker deposits the buyer's check into his trust account. The check clears the trust account.

The offer is not accepted by the seller. The broker then withdraws the buyer's good faith deposit from the trust account and deposits the funds in his personal account. From his personal account, the broker writes checks using the buyer's funds to pay personal expenses.

Is the broker's personal use of the buyer's funds cause for revocation or suspension of his license?

Yes! Not only has the broker violated the rule against commingling trust funds and personal funds, he has also *converted* the buyer's funds to his own use. Both violations are separate grounds for revocation or suspension of the broker's license. [**Brown v. Gordon** (1966) 240 CA2d 659]

Maintaining trust account integrity

Records maintained by the broker for his trust accounts both document and track the broker's **receipt and disbursement** of trust funds he receives. However, recordkeeping alone will not protect the broker against dishonest employees.

The assurance all trust funds are deposited into the trust account to the credit of the proper persons and disbursed or transferred as instructed by the owner of the funds and third parties who have an interest in the funds is best accomplished by maintaining a written journal or computerized accounting system. However, even the best of accounting procedures does not protect against deliberate diversion and defalcation of trust funds by others.

The broker named as trustee on a trust fund account is responsible for funds held in the account, even if others sign on the account with authorization to make withdrawals from the account. [DRE Reg. §2834(c)]

Occasionally, it is unfeasible for the broker to personally enter and maintain each accounting transaction and conduct the reconciliation required by the DRE. However, the broker can protect the trust funds in the trust account from unauthorized withdrawals by personally receiving, opening and reviewing bank statements and the paid checks returned with the statement before anyone else has access to the statements.

Banks and other depositories send a monthly statement of the account to each account holder for the purpose of verifying the validity of the deposits, withdrawals and charges on the account.

The broker, to maintain the integrity of the trust account, must make sure the statement is:

- mailed to the broker's office and handed to him unopened;

- held by the bank and picked up by the broker personally; or

- sent to the broker's residence instead of the office.

If unauthorized withdrawals from the account occur, the broker will likely discover the unauthorized withdrawals by reviewing the bank statement and the accompanying deposit tickets and paid checks before anyone else has access to the statement.

Should the broker discover any unauthorized withdrawals due to forgeries or improper endorsements, the broker must notify the bank within 30 days of receiving the statement. The notice of improper payment of checks by the bank will enable the broker to recover the amount of the unauthorized payment from the bank. [Calif. Commercial Code §4406]

Any loss from the trust account not covered by the bank must be covered by the broker — the person ultimately responsible for the account. Ultimately, to protect the broker from unrecoverable losses, business insurance must include coverage for employee theft.

Preparing the Interest-Bearing Trust Agreement

Identification: Enter the date and place the trust account agreement is prepared. This date is the date used to reference the agreement. **Enter** the name of the broker and the name of the owner of the trust funds.

Agreement:

1. *Deposit amount:* **Enter** the dollar amount of trust funds handed to the broker.

   1.1 *Related real estate agreement:* **Enter** the title given to the real estate related agreement under which the owner deposited the funds towards his performance, the date the agreement was entered into and the name of any other party to the agreement.

2. *Interest-bearing account:* **Enter** the name of the financial institution with whom the trust account will be opened for deposit of the trust funds. **Enter** the financial institution's address.

   2.1 *Name of the account:* **Check** the appropriate box to indicate who is the beneficiary of the trust funds. If the beneficiary is other than the owner, **enter** the name of the third party.

   2.2 *FDIC insured account:* The funds in the account are insured by the FDIC.

   2.3 *Type of account:* **Check** the appropriate box to indicate the type of interest-bearing account to be used, and if necessary, **enter** the name of the account.

   2.4 *Interest rate:* **Enter** the rate of interest to accrue on the account.

   2.5 *Compounding:* **Check** the appropriate box to indicate the period for compounding the interest on the account.

   2.6 *Service charge:* **Check** the appropriate box to indicate whether a service charge will be incurred on the account.

   2.7 *Disbursement of interest:* **Check** the appropriate box to indicate whether interest earned on the account will be paid to the owner or to another party. If the interest is not to be paid to the owner, **enter** the name of the party who is to receive the interest. **Enter** the event which triggers the payment of interest.

   2.8 *Withdrawal penalties:* **Enter** the number of days after deposit or the number of days' notice required for early withdrawal of the trust funds. **Enter** the amount of penalty for early withdrawal.

3. *Single-purpose account:* No other funds are to be deposited into this account.

4. *Account number:* **Enter** the account number.

    4.1   Authorization for the broker to enter the account number on opening the account called for in this agreement.

5. *Interested parties:* All persons with an interest in the funds which are the deposit placed in the interest bearing account must also consent to this agreement.

Signatures:

Broker's signature: **Enter** the date the broker signs the trust agreement. **Enter** the broker's name or the name of the agent acting on behalf of the broker. **Obtain** the broker's or agent's signature.

Owner's signature: **Enter** the date the owner signs the agreement. **Enter** the owner's name and social security number. **Obtain** the owner's signature.

Third party's signature: **Enter** the date the third party signs the agreement. **Enter** the name of the third party. **Obtain** the third party's signature.

Chapter 5

Trust fund accounting

This chapter discusses the accounting required for all deposited and undeposited trust funds.

Trust account bookkeeping

The broker's bookkeeping records for **each trust account** maintained at a bank or thrift must include entries regarding:

- the amount, date of receipt and source of all trust funds received;

- the date the trust funds were deposited in the broker's trust account;

- the date and check number for each disbursement of trust funds previously deposited in the trust account; and

- the daily balance of the trust account. [Department of Real Estate Regulation §2831(a)]

Entries in the **general ledger** for the overall trust account must be in chronological order of occurrences and formatted in columns. Also, the ledgers may be maintained in either a written journal or one generated by a computer program. [DRE Reg. §2831(c)]

In addition to the general ledger of the entire trust account, the broker must also maintain a separate **subaccount ledger** for each owner of trust funds. The subaccount ledger lists each deposit and disbursement from the broker's trust account on behalf of each owner of trust funds.

The separate, individual subaccount ledger must identify the parties (buyer/seller, tenant/landlord) to each entry, and include:

- the date and amount of trust funds **deposited**;

- the date, check number and amount of each **disbursement** from the trust account;

- the date and amount of any **interest earned** on funds in the trust fund account; and

- the total amount of trust **funds remaining** after each deposit or disbursement from the trust account. [DRE Reg. §2831.1]

Like the general ledger for the entire trust account, entries in each individual owner's subaccount ledger must also be in chronological order of occurrence and formatted in columns and maintained in a written journal or generated by a computer program. [DRE Reg. §2831.1(b)]

Undeposited trust funds

The broker will maintain a **trust fund record**, separate from his bank trust account, with a *ledger* identifying:

- the location (for safekeeping) of any trust funds received but not deposited in the trust account; and

- the date the funds were returned or forwarded, such as a check, cashier's check, cash or promissory note that is not deposited in the broker's trust account.

For example, a broker or his agent receives a check from a buyer as a good faith deposit on an offer to purchase real estate. The check is made payable to escrow.

Since the check is not made payable to the broker, the broker cannot negotiate or deposit the check into his trust account.

Thus, the broker makes no entry in his bank trust account record regarding the item received. The broker does, however, make an entry in his trust funds ledger on the date he received the check.

The check is retained by the broker. For safekeeping, the check is placed in the transaction file with all the other documents regarding the transaction.

The offer is timely accepted. The broker delivers the check to the escrow company to whom it is made payable. Again, he makes an entry in the trust funds ledger on the date the check was delivered to escrow.

Must the broker keep a record of his handling of a check he receives that is made payable to and delivered to escrow or anyone else?

Yes! The check represents trust funds temporarily entrusted to the broker by the buyer who signed and handed the offer to the broker acting in his capacity as a licensed agent. Thus, as trust funds, the check must be accounted for by the broker in his trust fund records — not in his trust account records.

When trust funds are not deposited in the broker's trust account, the broker must keep a separate record to account for having **received and delivered** the undeposited trust funds. [DRE Reg. §2831(a)(6)]

Conversely, a broker is not required to keep records of checks made payable to others for services, such as escrow, credit reports and appraisal services, if the total amount of all such checks for any one transaction does not exceed $1,000. [DRE Reg. §2831(e)]

However, on request from the Department of Real Estate (DRE) or the maker of the check exempt from entry in the trust fund ledger, the broker must account for the receipt and distribution of the check. Copies of all receipts must be retained for three years. [DRE Reg. §2831(e)]

All records of trust funds must be retained by the broker for **three years** after the closing or cancellation of the transaction involving the trust funds. [Calif. Business and Professions Code §10148(a)]

Further, lack of proper accounting records is evidence of negligence and incompetence in performing the broker's duties — grounds for suspension or revocation of the broker's license. [**Apollo Estates, Inc.** v. **Department of Real Estate** (1985) 174 CA3d 625]

Monthly reconciliation

Brokers maintaining bank trust accounts must compare and reconcile, at least once each calendar month during which deposits or withdrawals occur, the general ledger for the entire trust account against the separate subaccount ledger of each person and each transaction in the subaccounts.

The monthly reconciliation of the bank trust account prepared and maintained by the broker must contain:

- the name of the bank or thrift where the trust account is located and the account number;

- the date of the reconciliation;

- the account number of each subaccount in the trust account documenting the deposits, withdrawals and disbursement for each person; and

- the amount of funds remaining held in trust on behalf of each. [DRE Reg. §2831.2]

The use of a computer program for entry of transactional data and control of the various trust account ledgers reduces the multiple entries required of manual systems for data control.

Shortages and overages

A broker is instructed by an individual to disburse funds from the broker's trust account. The account contains trust funds belonging to more than one client. The disbursement, if made, would reduce the balance in the individual's separate subaccount ledger to below the amount of the trust funds remaining in the individual's subaccount, called a *negative balance*.

Sufficient funds are in the trust account to cover the disbursement if a check were written.

However, on reconciliation, the broker will be *out of trust*, since one individual has overdrawn his funds in the amount of the negative balance.

The broker, however, may issue the check for the overdraw if he first obtains written authorization from each person who has or is entitled to funds in the trust account. [DRE Reg. §2832.1]

In calculating the balance of the trust funds held in the bank trust account, only the remaining funds held for each individual in their subaccount are considered. Funds owned by one individual cannot be used to offset a negative balance in another individual's subaccount. [DRE Reg. §2832.1]

Unexplained overage ownership

Occasionally, the amount of all funds held in a trust account exceed the amount of trust funds held in all the subaccounts for individuals. The excess, however, is not the broker's commingled funds. An overage occurs when the broker cannot determine who is the owner of the excess funds, called *unexplained trust account overages*.

The overage generally arises due to mathematical errors in the entry of deposits or withdrawals, bank records, or failure to identify the owner of the funds when deposited or withdrawn and entered in the trust account records.

Unexplained excess funds — overages — in a trust account are still trust funds, even though the ownership of the funds cannot be determined.

An unexplained overage may not be withdrawn for the broker's business or personal use, or used to offset shortages on individual subaccounts in the trust account.

Excess funds are not the broker's funds since the broker cannot demonstrate he has instructions to withdraw the excess funds. The broker does not know who owns the funds to give the instructions for withdrawal.

Unexplained trust account overages must remain in the trust account, or be placed in a separate trust fund account established to hold unexplained overages.

Ultimately, the excess funds escheat to the state, unless the ownership of the unexplained overage is determined within three years of the discovery of the overage. [Calif. Code of Civil Procedure §1500 et seq.]

Trust account ledgers

To comply with trust accounting regulations, a broker, in addition to retaining all receipts for funds, deposit slips and checks issued, must maintain ledgers detailing:

- trust funds deposited and disbursed from the bank trust account, called a *general ledger* [See Figure 1];

- a separate record of trust funds received and disbursed on behalf of each individual, called a *subaccount ledger* [See Figure 2]; and

- trust funds received that are not deposited in the broker's trust account, called an *undeposited trust fund ledger*. [See Figure 3]

The maintenance of the ledgers is necessary not only for the broker's business use, but must be made available to the DRE in the event of an audit of the broker's trust accounts.

Computer programs have been developed that allow the broker to make a single entry for the receipt and disbursement of trust funds from the trust account under an account number given to the owner of the funds, called a *beneficiary*.

On completing the entry, the program automatically generates reports for the overall trust account, each owner's subaccount, and the statements to be sent to each owner of trust funds.

Sample transaction

Consider a broker who opens his bank trust account with a $100 deposit from his own funds to cover bank service charges. This deposit is entered by the broker on his overall trust account general ledger and on the broker's subaccount for his *appropriately commingled funds*. [See Figures 1 and 2]

The broker has three clients: Borrower One (BR1), Seller One (SE1) and Buyer One (BY1).

Borrower One retains the broker to arrange financing. The broker receives $300 from Borrower One to cover costs to be incurred for placing the loan, including appraisal and credit report costs.

These funds are deposited in the broker's trust account. The broker enters information on the deposit to Borrower One's subaccount under an account number assigned to Borrower One by the broker. [See Figure 4]

The entry is also recorded in the general ledger for the trust account as the general ledger is the balance of all the individual subaccounts.

Seller One enters into an exclusive seller's listing agreement with the broker and advances the broker $500 to cover costs to be incurred by the broker in marketing the seller's real estate as noted on a listing package advance cost sheet attached to the listing agreement. The broker deposits the $500 in his trust account. The information is then entered in a subaccount ledger under an account number assigned to Seller One by the broker. The balance is then entered in the general ledger.

Buyer One makes a purchase offer, and hands the broker a $1,000 check for a good faith deposit. Buyer One also advances the broker $500 to cover the cost of a property inspection, credit report and appraisal necessary to secure a loan to finance the purchase.

Figure 1

State Bank Account Number 123456789
Trust Account General Ledger
10/1/2004 to 10/5/2004

Date Rec.	Chk./Dep. Date	Chk. No.	Deposit/Pay to	Client	Source	Clear	Amount	Balance
			Beginning Balance					$ 0.00
10/1/04	10/1/04	N/A	Initial Deposit	Broker	Broker	Yes	$100.00	$100.00
10/1/04	10/1/04	N/A	Appraisal, credit report fee for loan	BR 1	BR 1	Yes	$300.00	$400.00
10/1/04	10/1/04	N/A	Advance costs	SE 1	SE 1	Yes	$500.00	$900.00
10/3/04	10/1/04	N/A	Appraisal, credit report and property inspection	BY 1	BY 1	Yes	$500.00	$1,400.00
N/A	10/3/04	1173	TRW Credit Reporting Service	BR 1	N/A	No	-$25.00	$1,375.00
N/A	10/3/04	1174	Appraiser service	BR 1	N/A	No	- $275.00	$1,100.00
N/A	10/5/04	1175	Appraiser service	BY 1	N/A	No	- $275.00	$825.00
N/A	10/5/04	1176	Home inspection service	BY 1	N/A	No	- $200.00	$625.00
N/A	10/5/04	1177	TRW Credit Reporting Service	BY 1	N/A	No	-$25.00	$600.00
N/A	10/5/04	1178	Local paper	SE 1	N/A	No	- $250.00	$350.00
N/A	10/5/04	1179	Local caterer	SE 1	N/A	No	- $100.00	$250.00

Figure 2
State Bank Account Number 123456789
Trust Account Subaccount Ledger

Date Rec. Date Dep.	Chk. No.	Deposit/Pay to Additional Description	Source Cleared	Amount	Running Balance
Subaccount 1					
> > > Client No. BROKER – Broker . . . Client Balance As Of . . . 10/1/2004					$ 0.00
10/1/04 10/1/04	N/A	Initial Deposit	Broker Yes	$ 100.00	$ 100.00
Subaccount 2					
> > > Client No. BR1 – Borrower 1 . . . Client Balance As Of . . . 10/1/2004					$ 0.00
10/1/04 10/1/04	N/A	Appraisal and credit report fee for loan on 124 University, Riverside	BR1 Yes	$ 300.00	$ 300.00
N/A 10/3/04	1173	TRW Credit Reporting Service Statement 10/2/01	N/A No	$ (25.00)	$ 275.00
N/A 10/3/04	1174	Appraiser Service Invoice #7654	N/A No	$ (275.00)	$ 0.00
Subaccount 3					
> > > Client No. SE1 – Seller 1 . . . . . Client Balance As Of . . . 10/1/2004					$ 0.00
10/1/04 10/1/04	N/A	Advance costs to sell property 125 Main Street, Riverside	SE1 Yes	$ 500.00	$500.00
N/A 10/5/04	1178	Local paper statement dated 10/3/01	N/A No	$ (250.00)	$ 250.00
N/A 10/5/04	1179	Local caterer statement dated 10/3/01	N/A No	$ (100.00)	$ 150.00
Subaccount 4					
> > > Client No. BY1 – Buyer . . . . . . Client Balance As Of . . . 10/1/2004					$ 0.00
10/3/04 10/3/04	N/A	Advance costs for purchase of property located at 123 university, Riverside	BY1 No	$ 500.00	$ 500.00
N/A 10/5/04	1175	Appraiser Service for property located at 123 university, Riverside	N/A No	$ (275.00)	$ 225.00
N/A 10/5/04	1176	Home inspector Service Invoice #7654	N/A No	$ (200.00)	$ 25.00
N/A 10/5/04	1177	TRW Credit Reporting Service Invoice #1123	N/A No	$ (25.00)	$ 0.00

Figure 3

RECORD OF ALL TRUST FUNDS RECEIVED –
NOT PLACED IN BROKER'S TRUST ACCOUNT
(Includes Notes and Uncashed Checks and Valuables Taken As Deposits)

2004 Date Recv'd	Form of Receipt (Cash, etc.)	Amount	Recv'd From	Description of Property or Other Identification	Disposition of Funds (To escrow, principle trust account, or return)	Date of Disptn
10/1/04	Check	$1,000	Buyer 1	123 University Riverside	To escrow company	10/5/04

Figure 4

State Bank – 123456789
Statement for Borrower's Account No. Borrower – BR1

Date Rec. Date Dep.	Check No.	Deposit/Pay to Additional Description	Source Cleared	Amount	Amount Balance
10/1/04 10/1/04	N/A	Appraisal and credit report loan fee for 124 University, Riverside	BR 1 Yes	$ 300.00	$ 300.00
N/A 10/3/04	1173	TRW Credit Reporting Service Statement 10/2/01	N/A No	$ (25.00)	$ 275.00
N/A 10/3/04	1174	Appraiser service Invoice #7654	N/A No	$ (275.00)	$ 0.00

The broker is instructed by Buyer One not to negotiate the $1,000 good faith deposit check until the offer is accepted. The $500 is deposited in the broker's trust account and entered in a subaccount ledger under an account number assigned to Buyer One by the broker, and entered on the trust account general ledger. The $1,000 check is held undeposited, but is entered on the broker's ledger for undeposited trust funds. [See Figure 3]

The overall balance of the broker's trust account is now $1,400. The balances of the subaccounts within the trust account are:

- $100 in Account 1, representing the broker's initial deposit in the account to cover account fees;

- $300 in Account 2, representing the funds received by the broker from Borrower One;

- $500 in Account 3, representing the funds received by the broker from Seller One; and

- $500 in Account 4, representing the $500 received by the broker from Buyer One (the $1,000 check held undeposited by the broker as instructed by Buyer One is not part of the balance of the broker's trust account).

The broker then pays out $25 for a credit report and $275 for an appraisal for Borrower One in Subaccount 2.

These disbursements are entered on both Borrower One's subaccount ledger and the general ledger.

The information from the subaccount ledger for Account 2 will be used to generate Borrower One's monthly statement from the broker. [See Figure 4]

Buyer One's purchase offer is accepted by the owner of the real estate, and the broker delivers Buyer One's check for the $1,000 good faith deposit to escrow (as payee or by endorsement). The broker records the transfer of the check on the broker's separate ledger for undeposited trust funds. [See Figure 3]

From the trust account, the broker also disburses $275 for an appraisal of the property, $200 for an inspection of the property and $25 for a credit report on Buyer One.

These disbursements are entered by the broker on Buyer One's subaccount ledger, and the trust account general ledger.

On behalf of Seller One, the broker disburses $250 for advertising and $100 to hold an open house. These disbursements are also entered on the subaccount ledger and the general ledger.

All three transactions close without further disbursements. What is the current balance of the trust account?

A $250 balance now exists in the broker's trust account. The balances of the subaccounts are:

- $100 in Subaccount 1, the broker's initial deposit of his own funds to open the trust account;

- $0 in Subaccount 2, as the funds received from Borrower One were completely exhausted;

- $150 in Subaccount 3, representing the remainder of the funds received by the broker from Seller One; and

- $0 in Subaccount 4, as the funds received from Buyer One were completely exhausted.

Any funds remaining in the subaccounts after the transactions have closed are not the property of the broker and must be returned to their owner, as well as an accounting in the form of a statement on the owner's subaccount.

Chapter
6

Penalties for misuse of trust funds

This chapter examines the penalties which may be incurred by brokers and their agents for the mishandling of trust funds.

Commingling, conversion and restitution

A California real estate broker who handles funds entrusted to him by others must deposit the trust funds as instructed by the owner of the funds.

Above all, a broker must not *convert* to his personal use any funds entrusted to him.

The trust fund handling requirements are backed up by a variety of **penalties** and **consequences** that apply to a broker who misuses trust funds, including:

- civil liability for money wrongfully converted;

- disciplinary action by the Department of Real Estate (DRE);

- income tax liability; and

- criminal sanctions for embezzlement.

The penalties depend partly on the nature of the funds which the broker misuses. For example, penalties for a broker's misuse of **advance fees** held in trust accounts are specifically fixed by statute.

The advance-fee statute allows a client to recover treble damages plus attorney fees from a broker who mishandles advance fees. Also, a broker who fails to account for advance fees is presumed to be guilty of embezzlement. [Calif. Business and Professions Code §10146]

However, the existence of specific statutory provisions relating to the misuse of advance fees does not mean the misuse of other types of trust funds will go unpunished. Penalties for the misuse of trust funds for other purposes fall under more general statutory schemes.

DRE discipline

If the DRE commissioner determines a broker has or is about to violate trust fund accounting rules, the commissioner may file an action and obtain an injunction against the broker to stop or prevent the violation. [B & P C §10081.5]

In the action, the commissioner may include a claim for *restitution* on behalf of individuals injured by the broker's actions. [B & P C §10081(b)]

Also, if the DRE conducts an audit of the broker's trust account and discovers the broker has *commingled* or *converted* to his own use more than $10,000 of trust funds, the broker's license may be suspended pending a formal hearing.

After the hearing, a receiver may be appointed to oversee the broker's business. The receiver is allowed to exercise any power the broker may have had and may file a bankruptcy petition on behalf of the broker. [B & P C §10081.5]

Inappropriate commingling of trust funds is grounds for suspension or revocation of the broker's license. [B & P C §10176(e)]

Civil liability

At the very least, a broker who misuses trust funds must **reimburse** the owner of the funds for the amount wrongfully converted. Any person who is deprived of property entrusted to a broker is entitled to recover an amount of money that will compensate him for the loss. [Calif. Civil Code §3281]

However, a principal's right to recover money from a broker who misuses trust funds is not limited to the amount or value of the funds the broker has wrongfully converted.

The principal, in addition to money losses, can be awarded punitive penalties based on a breach of the broker's agency relationship with the client. Also, when a broker acts as the principal's agent and uses the principal's money for his own benefit, any **profits earned** by the broker's misuse of the funds are presumed to belong to the principal.

Thus, the principal is entitled to **recover the funds** wrongfully converted, **plus any gain** the broker has derived from the use of the funds. [**Savage** v. **Mayer** (1949) 33 C2d 548]

For example, a broker representing a seller of real estate presents the property to a buyer at a price exceeding the seller's listing price. The buyer signs an offer to purchase at the price solicited by the broker and gives him a good faith deposit.

However, the broker never communicates the buyer's offer to the seller. Instead, the broker purchases the property from the seller at the seller's lower listed price, then deeds the property to the buyer. The broker keeps the difference between the listed price and the purchase price as a profit.

The buyer seeks to recover from the broker the money difference between the price he paid the broker and the price the broker paid the seller. The broker claims the buyer is not entitled to recover the difference since the property acquired was worth at least what the buyer paid for it.

However, the buyer's recovery is not limited to actual losses since the broker used the buyer's deposit to secretly make a profit for himself. Thus, the buyer is entitled to recover the profits realized by the broker. [**Ward** v. **Taggart** (1959) 51 C2d 736]

Additionally, a broker who wrongfully converts trust funds may be liable for **punitive damages**. Punitive damages, also called *exemplary damages*, is a money award given to a principal when the broker has wrongfully obtained assets, such as trust funds, from the principal by fraud or with malice. [CC §3294]

Any wrongful use of trust funds is automatically fraudulent since the broker's breach of his agency duty is defined by statute as constructive fraud. [CC §1573]

Thus, any broker misusing trust funds is potentially liable to the principal for punitive damages as well as reimbursement of the trust funds taken or misused. Whether punitive damages will be awarded depends on the severity of the broker's misconduct and the agency relationship undertaken by the broker.

For example, a seller and a broker enter into a listing agreement that employs the broker to sell a property. Under the listing, the broker's fee will be any amount paid by a buyer in excess of the net sales price sought by the seller.

After the seller signs the listing agreement, the broker alters the fee provision to provide for a brokerage fee of one third of the sales proceeds.

The broker accepts cash funds from a buyer for the full sales price of the property. The broker handles the closing and retains one third of the sales proceeds as his brokerage fee. The balance handed to the seller is an amount less than the net amount agreed to by the seller in the listing agreement.

Here the seller is entitled to punitive damages based not only on the wrongful conversion of gross sales proceeds held in trust for the seller, but on the broker's fraudulent conduct. The broker could not honestly believe he was entitled to a fee equal to one third of the sales proceeds. [**Haigler** v. **Donnelly** (1941) 18 C2d 674]

In cases where actual money losses are small, punitive money awards are sometimes awarded as a deterrent to future fraudulent activity. [**Esparza** v. **Specht** (1976) 55 CA3d 1]

Also, the broker who misappropriates **advance fees** can be held liable for a money award up to three times the amount of the missing trust funds, plus interest and attorney fees. [B & P C §10146; CC §3287]

The Real Estate Recovery Account

If an individual sues a broker for trust account violations and receives a judgment, the individual can satisfy the judgment through the state Real Estate Recovery Account if:

- the broker is insolvent; and

- the losses are directly related to the broker's conduct.

However, the individual's recovery is limited to $20,000 per transaction and is further limited to actual losses on the transaction which resulted from broker fraud. [B & P C §10471 et seq.]

For example, an owner of income-producing real estate enters into a property management agreement with a broker.

Under the property management agreement, the broker collects rents from the tenants and arranges and pays for maintenance of the real estate. The owner gives the broker a cash advance to cover maintenance expenses.

The broker deposits the cash advance into his personal account. Tenants pay their rents to the broker in cash. The cash is also deposited into the broker's personal checking account. The broker then issues a check on his personal account payable to the owner for all funds due the owner.

The check is rejected by the broker's bank due to insufficient funds. The owner demands that the broker pay him for the rents collected and return the cash advanced for maintenance, or account for the funds if they have been disbursed.

The broker refuses to account to the owner. The owner sues the broker and is awarded a judgment for:

- three times the amount of **rents collected** by the broker and not paid to the owner;

- three times the amount of the **cash advanced** for maintenance, as no evidence exists showing the broker expended the funds for the benefit of the owner;

- **pre-judgment** interest at the legal rate (10%) on the rents and cash advanced from the date they were received by the broker;

- post-judgment interest (10%) until the judgment is satisfied;

- costs; and

- attorney fees.

The owner attempts to collect on the judgment but is unable to do so since the broker is insolvent.

Can the owner collect all of his judgment against the broker for the misuse of trust funds from the Real Estate Recovery Account?

No! The owner can only recover his *actual and direct* losses on the transaction from the Recovery Account, up to the sum of $20,000. Thus, the owner's recovery is not only limited by the $20,000 ceiling, but is limited to the actual amount of his lost rents and the cash advanced for maintenance. The tripled amount cannot be recovered from the Recovery Account because the amount exceeds the actual loss inflicted by the broker. [**Circle Oaks Sales Co.** v. **Real Estate Commissioner** (1971) 16 CA3d 682]

Also, no attorney fees award can be recovered from the Recovery Account since attorney fees are not direct losses. [**Acebo** v. **Real Estate Education, Research and Recovery Fund** (1984) 155 CA3d 907]

However, the owner can recover the interest and court costs awarded in the judgment from the Recovery Account as part of the $20,000 maximum recovery. [**Nordahl** v. **Franzalia** (1975) 48 CA3d 657]

Income tax

Taxes must be paid on all income, from whatever source, including income derived from illegal activities such as embezzlement. [**James** v. **United States** (1961) 366 US 213]

Thus, a broker who converts trust funds to his personal use exposes himself to tax penalties if he fails to report the converted funds as income and pay the appropriate taxes on the *illegal income*. [Calif. Revenue and Taxation Code §19701]

Further, embezzled money must be reported as income even if it is paid back. Thus, a broker **embezzling trust funds** cannot escape income tax liability by returning the funds and characterizing the embezzlement as an unauthorized loan. [**Buff** v. **Commissioner of Internal Revenue** (1974) 496 F2d 847]

In addition, no deductions of any kind are allowed to offset income derived from illegal activities. The broker is responsible for reporting the **full amount** of the income he has derived from converting trust funds, undiminished by his related expenses, costs and reimbursements. [Rev & T C §17282]

Embezzlement

A broker who uses funds entrusted to him for any purpose other than as authorized may be held guilty of embezzlement. [Calif. Penal Code §506]

Whether the broker is merely "borrowing" the funds and intends to return them is of no import. The return of the misused funds may be a factor mitigating the broker's sentence, but he is still guilty of embezzlement. [Pen C §513]

For instance, a developer accepts down payments from buyers for homes in a subdivision. The purchase agreements state the down payments will be held in escrow until title to the homes is conveyed to the buyers.

However, the developer fails to deposit any of the funds received into an escrow or trust account. Instead, the developer uses the funds for his own business expenses.

The developer gives the buyers credit for the down payments received and later conveys title to the buyers. Thus, the buyers are not harmed by the developer's conversion of the down payments to his own personal or business use. However, the funds the developer accepted were not his to use as his own, but were to be held in trust for the buyers.

Even though the down payments are meant to ultimately go to the developer, and the buyers received what they paid for, the developer has no right under the purchase agreements to use the funds until he conveys title. Thus, the developer is guilty of embezzlement. [**People** v. **Parker** (1965) 235 CA2d 100]

The *Parker* case involves a developer, not a broker. However, the same reasoning would apply to a broker's misuse of trust funds. Further, an embezzlement charge against a broker would be stronger since a major element of embezzlement is the breach of an agency or fiduciary relationship.

Finally, the broker who fails to account for advance fees is presumed to have embezzled the funds. [B & P C §10146]

For example, a broker is hired by a borrower to arrange a loan. The borrower hands the broker a check for advance fees for locating a lender. The advance fee check is deposited in the broker's trust account.

However, the broker fails to keep any record of the receipt or disbursement of trust funds from the trust account. The loan is never arranged and the borrower demands the return of the advance. The broker refuses, claiming the borrower's funds have been properly spent.

Is the broker required to return the advanced funds?

Yes! Even if the broker did not misuse any of the funds in the trust account, the broker is **presumed** to have misappropriated the funds since he failed to retain any record of the deposit or disbursements from the trust account and is unable to prove the money was not misappropriated. [**Burch** v. **Argus Properties, Inc.** (1979) 92 CA3d 128]

Case Index

California Attorney General Opinion

California Code Index

Federal Code Index

Topical Index

E

F

G

General account (See Trust account)

Good faith 11

    closing costs 11

    deposits 11

L

Lender

    lender disclosure statement 33

    liability 111

    loan brokerage 33

    loan terms 37

Loan brokerage 25

    disclosures

    inducing a borrow to employ 25

    lender disclosure statement

    loan terms 30,31,37

    private lender 33

    property conditions 36

    marketing "free services" 25,26

M

Misrepresentations 4

    ability to pay 34

    employment 8

    for personal gain 4

    loan terms 30,31

    potential use of property 19,20

    property conditions 5,17-24

    real estate values 4,5

    unconditional representations 6

Multiple Listing Service (MLS)

    marketing information 19

    membership and agency 61

O

Office management

    broker use of supervisors 71

    liability 75

Owner's statement

P

Property disclosures 5

    approximations

    "as is" provision 17,18

    failure to disclose 17,18,19

    boundaries 18

    potential use 19,20

    public record investigation 23,24

    seller's representations 18,22,23

    size 18

    title conditions 18,21,23,24

R

Real estate law 3

Rules of Agency (See Agency)

S

Sales agent (See Agent)

T